A Slap of the Hand

The History of Hereford Market

Editor: Bill Laws
Additional research: Bobbie Blackwell

'In those days a slap of the hand and the deal was done'

Herefordshire Lore in association with **Logaston Press**

Herefordshire Lore
www.herefordshirelore.org.uk
in association with
Logaston Press
Little Logaston Woonton Almeley
Herefordshire HR3 6QH
www.logastonpress.co.uk

First published by Herefordshire Lore & Logaston Press 2007; reprinted 2007, 2008
Copyright © text: Herefordshire Lore 2007
Copyright © illustrations: as per acknowledgements

ISBN 978 1 904396 85 7

Typeset in by Logaston Press
and printed in Great Britain by Bell & Bain Ltd., Glasgow

Front cover illustration: October 1956 and the start of a busy two-day cattle sale at Hereford Market. Auctioneer Bill Gallimore holds the gavel with Frank Robinson and Frank Russell in the rostrum. The cattle belonged to Baden Powell from Whitney-on-Wye. Two of the porters are George Matthews and Reg Wall. (Brightwells)

A Slap of the Hand
The History of Hereford Market

Contents

Herefordshire Lore works to remember, celebrate and record Herefordshire's past before it is lost with the passing of the generations. Herefordshire Lore has been collecting and publishing people's memories since 1989, working closely with Herefordshire Archive Service, Herefordshire Libraries and Museums, and Age Concern. A copy of all the interviews carried out by Herefordshire Lore is lodged with the Herefordshire Archive Service.

This book is dedicated to all those who worked in the markets.

Acknowledgements

The material for this book is based on the recollections of many. We are especially grateful to them and to all those who helped with the book: Neil Adams, Graham Baker, Michael Ball, Peter Bayliss, Reg Bayliss, Margaret Bell, Fay Bowen, Nigel Bowen, Percy Bristow, Colin Breen, Bert Brookes, Harry Carroll, Ron Chatburn, Terry Court, C.H. Davies, Maisey and Phyliss Farr, Julian Gallimore, Don Gleed, Ted Green, Richard Hall, Cyril Harris, John Harris, Margaret and Dennis Hobby, Eve Huskins, Eric and Wendy Jones, Geoff Jones, Ken Lyke, Elsie Lloyd, John and Elsie Lloyd, John Matthews, Frances Mathews, Frank Morgan, Geoffrey Morgan-Jones, Colin Manning, Tom Nellist, A.J. Pearce, David Probert, Joanne Probert, David Prothero and the Hereford Cattle Society, Ray Pudge, Andy Rutherford, Bill Sayce, Paul Sevenoaks, Hilary Smallwood, Colin and Margaret Smith, June Smith, Lillian Smith, John Stevens, Paula Taylor, Chris and Irene Tomlinson, Rosemarie Watkins, Ken Webb, Tom and Margaret Wheatstone, Mrs S. Winney, Robin Hill and staff at Herefordshire Libraries and Museums, and Herefordshire County Archives.

Thanks too to the interviewers and Herefordshire Lore committee: Sandy Green, Mary Horner, Eileen Klotz, Sarah Laws, Rosemary Lillico, Eddie McEnery, Marsha O'Mahony, Harvey Payne, Elizabeth Semper O'Keefe, Dawn Turner, John Turner, Betty Webb and Lenora Williams.

This is a Heritage Lottery Project.

John Harris and Ted Green share their memories of Herefordshire Market with Sarah Laws.

Foreword

This book is the result of many people, some known to me, some not, telling numerous tales of Hereford Market during the early, middle and later years of the twentieth century. It is, if anything, a tribute to those who bought, sold or were otherwise involved in the two markets – Livestock and Butter; those farmers, dealers, traders, butchers, auctioneers and their staff, porters, drovers, hauliers, and their wives many of whom were actively involved as well. I may have missed some but not by intent.

I have enjoyed contributing in a small way to this book and there has been much telling of tales and reminiscing of people and events. It is not an in-depth history, although I was impressed as to how much the chapter on The Origins of the Market has enhanced my knowledge. It will, we can be sure, be used in years to come by future historians. The thought of all those hours of taped interviews now with the Herefordshire County Archives that will keep someone engaged for many hours.

I am not the oldest contributor to this book although my experience did start in the middle 1950s. I was the boy who ran the sale slips for 5s (Auctioneers - Walking the plank) and in my innocence was convinced that running meant just that. Having covered the 220 yards from Sale ring to Market Office and then back in what may have an under-16 record for 440 yards I was told by Jack Lyke: 'There's not that much rush, boy.'

A readable book that will bring back happy memories and, who knows, with new tales to tell may lead to a sequel.

Julian Gallimore

Farming Today – and Yesterday

Dealers, land owners, tenant farmers and smallholders large and small have used the city's markets to sell their produce since Norman times. Different contributors recall how Herefordshire is, and always was, a farming community.

ROGER THE BULL

People do have a wonderful relationship with stock. And they do treat them well. We know the animals go off and get put on your Sunday lunch table, but there is no reason why they can't be looked after in conditions which they deserve. (Factory farming gets me a bit cross.)

It had to be a hard life really because you were working such long hours. I left Woolhope School when I was 13 and went to work on Wessington Farm, Woolhope. I did everything on the farm, milking, the horses, driving the tractor, haymaking, corn harvest. In the winter you had to feed the horses twice a day. Some of these people who worked on big farms where they would keep fifteen horses, they used to have to start at 4.30 each morning. And then go to 10 p.m., feed the horses and back to bed. I had to start about 6.30 a.m. I'd been milking since I was about six on the local farm nearby. There was three of us milking and we'd do about five cows in an hour.

We used to grow mangels, sugar beet and they had to be hoed, separated out so they would grow bigger.

Got paid, oh yes, weren't very much! When I first started it was only five pence a week, and live in, because of the milking. We were very well looked after, never short of anything. Even through the war there was always plenty to eat.

When I finished with this farm at Woolhope I went to work at relief farm work and I'd been saving my money. I always wanted

Rattling his bag to move the sheep along, a haulier collects his flock. Hereford Market has been central to the life of the farming community. (Bobbie Blackwell)

to go on my own and bought this little 30 acre farm and it cost me £5,100. It was the best thing I did. Down here I started off selling milk and kept about 40 cows plus Roger the bull. And then I gave up the milk, went into calf rearing and store cattle. And then I suppose I got too old really to look after big cattle, and changed into sheep.

There is a huge range of farming in the county. In the early 1960s it was a boom time, a wonderful time for Hereford cattle particularly, so we didn't see a lot of hardship. Some of the bigger arable men and stockmen, farming two or three hundred acres, were doing very well indeed. But you'd also got your Black Mountain farmers who might have a lot of acres, but they're hill run. They were farming stock with no chance of any arable and they worked whatever hours were necessary, through from dawn to dusk. In the winter you're working from before dawn to after dusk to keep the cattle fed and make sure the sheep are all right.

Since then we've had problems. We've had a down turn in the agricultural industry. Some of the smaller farmers have had to take other jobs whereas there was a time when men milked cows on something like a 50 acre holding. They would work damn hard, but it was a living. A lot of those men have gone now. The holdings have been increased in size to be able to make a living.

WE WERE HAPPY

In the winter the cattle were in. And on Christmas Eve we always went round to look at the cattle the night before we went to bed, to see if they were all right.

It was something special.

One farmer I was talking to one day told me when he started he sold the piano out of the house to buy his first cow! Some farmers did well. No matter what business you talk about there are always some that make a lot of money and some that don't. You just got to be in the right thing at the right time.

We never asked for much and we didn't expect it then. We were happy, remembers *Fay Bowen*. She was brought up in Grosmont. Mum lost dad when I was four and my brother was two. Mum was strong. She'd been brought up on a farm and could turn her hand to anything. She wore ordinary, strong clothes. I never saw her in trousers. She'd make pinafores out of old bags of swede sacks to go in front of you.

She had cows and calves, cow for the house and some sheep, and some pigs to kill in the winter or in the autumn to eat in the winter, salt the ham in the cellar then hang the shoulders up.

We had 264 acres. I left school at 14 and came home and helped. I did anything going in the house in the morning — we

Shire foals at the Grange Farm, Kingstone, with Ken and Derek Winney in 1943. (Mrs S. Winney)

had no electric, just the wood fires with the oven on the side — and then I'd be out in the afternoon. I've raked hay up and mowed, worked with horses, and tractors when they came in the beginning of World War Two.

The day the evacuees came Mum took in two sisters and a brother that nobody wanted. They were good little children: Mum loved them. She always kept a good table so it was no trouble to feed them. They scrubbed the floors with me, churned the butter, and turned the handle for the shearing machine.

In the dairy she'd make butter and cheese, go to Abergavenny Market with it. When the butter was plentiful and you weren't selling it, you'd got to salt some down for winter. You just put it in these stone jars, put more salt in and it would keep all winter. It wouldn't go rancid. When we didn't have greaseproof paper we would sometimes wash a dock leaf and wrap the butter up in that.

We kept geese and ducks, and reared chickens, buy them a day old. We used to catch rabbits with ferrets and nets. From eight years old I used to shoot them with a .410.

We used to cut stakes and pea and bean sticks. Used to tush them out the woods with the pony and a tushing chain to sell. We youngsters could only manage a pony.

1951 Ken Winney of Kingstone Grange Farm came second at the Llanwarne Ploughing Match on his Fordson. This match is still held every autumn. (Mrs S. Winney)

Wagoner Arty Mills ploughing at the Wormbridge Vallets Farm annual ploughing match in the early 1950s. (Mrs S. Winney)

We did pick a lot of blackberries in the autumn when they were about, and we'd got good damson, apple and pear trees. We'd store the fruit through the winter, fill two or three bedrooms with the fruit in straw, making sure they didn't touch, and then take it to Market on a Tuesday and a Friday.

If we couldn't sell in Abergavenny Market we used to go to Hereford Market, in the Cattle Market or the Butter Market, to sell blackberries, sometimes, or peas out of the field, 'cause we always planted two or three rows of peas in the summer. You'd take a basket full to sell them.

Shearing down on the farm. Danzie Drew (right) from Lyonshall uses a hand-cranked shearing machine. Danzie, the brother of Hereford bonesetter Eddie Drew, travelled from farm to farm shearing sheep ready for the Market.
(Margaret & Dennis Hobby)

INTO MARKET

Rosemarie Watkins was brought up on a farm near Kilpeck.

The farm always came first. Cows was my favourite. We didn't have bulls. I remember walking a cow with my father up to the next farm. When we got the cow in the yard where the bull was I was sent home straight away so's I didn't see that! The cow seemed to come home easier than she went.

'Cause I never had a brother, I was the boy. I had to do anything on the farm. I remember one Christmas Day a school friend saying: 'What are you wearing Christmas Day?' I'll wear any old thing to go and take the silage out!

A farm sale at Robert Orgee's Church House Farm, Pencombe. Tom Price who owned a Cheltenham Gold Cup winner, Flaky Dove, is leaning on the gate. (Graham Baker)

I used to go to the Cattle Market with my father. Women didn't help so much then. On Market day we had to go down to Kilpeck and ring up Hubert Williams, he had a stock lorry. I remember going in the cattle lorry. I didn't get dressed up for market — there wasn't time for that. We didn't wear trousers: I expect I was wearing skirts.

Once we'd got the cattle off I'd drive them into the pens with a stick. You'd get some water in a bucket and clean their tails and see that their udders were clean. You'd talk to other people and go and have a bit of something to eat. We never had a proper meal, just a bun and a drink. Sometimes you'd go and treat yourself to fish and chips at Westwoods. Sometimes I'd sneak off to the shops because you usually wanted cheese and meat. We grew our own vegetables.

You knew what number you were and my father or I would go in near the auctioneers' rostrum and stand by it so they knew what your reserve was. I was a bit embarrassed about that, I don't know why. Dad usually took charge, but if for some reason he couldn't go to Market well, then I'd have to see to it. People helped each other. It was the understood thing.

Once when we were on holiday in the Lake District I said: 'Oh there's a farm sale there. Do you want to stop?' And my husband said: 'No. I don't know anybody.' 'Cause a big part of it was somebody to have a chat to. It was the social side.

HOP PICKING HOLIDAYS

My husband went to Garway School and I went to Orcop recalled *Lillian Smith*. I think they learnt more at Garway than we did at Orcop! When we walked home we used to eat things from the hedgerows, sweet briar, we used to suck the end of honeysuckle, and then there'd be wild strawberries and a square-shaped clover, a sort of sour taste. It was nice.

I used to walk the three and half miles down from Bagwyl-lydiart to the little market by the hall in Pontrilas. We used to take eggs down and buy cakes and bread. They used to sell all sorts of vegetables and chickens, and things like that. There was a bakery then, and we'd buy Chelsea buns and eat them on the way back.

Our summer holiday was a fortnight's hop picking. When I'd filled an upside-down umbrella twice we were allowed to go and play. I tell you what, an umbrella used to take some filling. We had people up from Wales, Kent, from all over the place. And the Travellers, the Gypsies, the Smiths and all them. We all got on.

You picked hops in your school holidays.
(Tom and Margaret Wheatstone)

COTTAGE LIFE

Frances James was born in 1915 at Ashburton Cottage on the Gloucester Road in Ross.

I lived there with my father, a house painter, my mother who took in washing, and my three sisters and one brother till I was fourteen and went into service.

We had a lot of freedom as children. We wore starched white pinafores, back to front, buttoned at the back, and lace up boots. I went to the Walter Scott School and on Saturdays I used to go and scrub someone's long passage. I got a shilling for that and my dinner.

We had two bedrooms and a kitchen. Down the passage was the wash boiler and a fire, and there was a lean-to where the coal was kept, and the tap house shared between the two cottages. That tap was all we had and our lavatory was under covers. Mum used to fill buckets of water. Bath day was quite a big job. We used to have a bath in one of those great long tin baths in front of the fire every Friday night.

We lived in the kitchen. We had one of these big wooden settles with a high back all the way up one side of the table and then we had the fire grate and we all sat round there. We used to sit round the fire sometimes and have our own musical evenings. My dad used to play the accordion and the violin. I didn't play anything. I was musical, but only in my head.

Left: Sizing her up. A Belgian Blue milking cow
goes under the hammer at the Market.
This beast was the first of its breed to be sold at
Hereford Cattle Market in 1975. (Graham Baker)

MURRAY MINTS

There were two fellows both worked on the Market and both called Ted Phipps and they were real characters. 'Curly' Ted Phipps lived in a barn on Aylestone Hill and liked a fight if he'd had a couple of pints.

They would move animals round the Market and they would sometimes partake too much ale and sleep in the market overnight next to a pen of cattle or pigs.

Lady Abel Smith from Tenbury — she was lady-in-waiting to the Queen — used to come and buy calves every Wednesday. The porter who used to sleep rough, in a barn off Aylestone Hill was highly intelligent (he could speak fluent French) but he didn't have a bath very frequently and he was followed everywhere by his dog, a collie on a piece of binder twine.

He would always load her calves. She would go with the payslip and say to him: 'I've got ten calves. Will you load them for me?' He always used to give her a sweet. I said to her once: 'I hope you don't mind me saying, but I can't really recommend those sweets. He lives in a barn and I don't think he's had a wash for a fortnight.'

'Ah,' she said, 'they're Murray Mints and they're always wrapped.'

THE BONE SETTER

Mr Drew seemed to know how to get your bones back into place. His whole family had this wonderful ability to sort out misplaced bones. Mr Drew was a short, stocky man who always wore a brown smock and a tweed cap. Very quiet, very reserved, very nice. On a Wednesday, to save the farmers going all the way out to Lyonshall to see him, he had a surgery, if that's the right word, in the Wheatsheaf in Newmarket Street. He used to rent this room and meet his clients in there over half a beer. Then he'd get them down on the table and straighten their back or their legs or their arms and probably charge them half a crown. You knew you were going to get some pain, but you knew ultimately that you'd be better. There was no medical assistance or medicines, just brute force.

He specialised in animals. If we had a problem in the Market we'd pop up and say: 'Mr Drew can you come down and look at this?'

Eddie Drew the bone setter had a way with people and animals.
(Margaret & Dennis Hobby)

Eddie Drew's mother, Margaret Drew, a direct descendant of Silver John Lloyd, outside their home at Lyonshall with Eddie's sister, Minnie, in the 1940s. (Margaret & Dennis Hobby)

SILVER JOHN

Eddie Drew inherited his skills from his famous but forgotten relative, Silver John Lloyd.

John Lloyd was credited with the ability to heal both man and beast. At the turn of the last century he lived with his wife on a small sheep farm in Radnor Forest by Harley Dingle under Great Creigiau, a few miles north of New Radnor.

After setting the spine of an injured miller's son, John was presented with a silver button by the grateful miller. He had refused money: 'I dunna take no gold or money for what the Almighty gave me.'

John's wife sewed the button onto the waistcoat her husband always wore to market. In time, as his reputation grew, so did the number of silver buttons sewn onto that waistcoat. Eventually both waistcoat and smock glittered like a coat of silver mail.

Then, one fateful night, John's pony and trap returned from Builth Market without the healer. A search of the district failed to find him.

The following winter the annual St Andrew's Fair was held on the frozen surface of Llynheilyn, a small lake near Forest Inn on the Builth to Kington road. But the festivities came to an abrupt halt when young Mary, the daughter of the Forest Inn landlord, let out a scream. There, beneath her feet and entombed in the ice, was the body of Silver John.

John had been murdered, some said by a gang of no-gooders from New Radnor, and dumped in the lake. His body was buried beneath Great Creigiau on a spot known ever afterwards as Silver John's Tump. No-one ever stood trial for the murder, but an old Radnor song goes:

> Silver John is dead and gone
> So they came a-singing.
> The Radnor boys pulled out his eyes
> And set the bells a ringing.

Marketing Memories

Market Day meant different things to different people. Various auctioneers, farmers and dealers recall what it meant to them.

MAN AND HIS ANIMALS

The Market is about the relationship between man and his animals. It is a wonderful relationship.

Peter Bayliss: Father used to ring the bell at the Market to start them off.

Reg Bayliss: They couldn't start the sale until I had permission from them to ring the bell every time, at the beginning of every sale. They could start then.

Hereford Market in the days when a slap of the hand sealed the deal. Auctioneer Colin Manning hands a trophy to Mr Davies of Duffrin, Wormbridge for his Champion Dairy Cow in 1955. (Graham Baker)

The Market was a fantastic place to be. Now it's nothing like it was then. We were having anything up to 3,000 or 4,000 fat sheep on a Monday. We'd have 500 pigs and 600 fat cattle, all on a Monday. Tuesday we'd have 600 bulls or 200 horses. On a Wednesday we'd have 12,000 sheep, 1,000 pigs, 600 calves, 500 weaning sturkie things — young cattle: there's calves, cows, cattle and then store cattle — and then on a Thursday we'd have anything up to 2,000 store cattle up to 600 barren cows and up to 400 dairy on a Friday so it was a busy old place.

The railway came up from Bulmer's where the big vats are now. There were sidings where the cattle trucks would put in. At the end of the sales we would be taking the cattle across the road under the leadership of the porter, Bunty Fletcher from Leominster, and loading.

We'd get customers coming from all over the United Kingdom. There were very few animals lorried then, they were all trained to various parts. This was before Beeching, of course.

Hereford was purely a market town.

There used to be queues everywhere. It was chaotic. They'd have what were called lairages. And in the one lairage, you'd have small pens for pigs. Sheep in another. There's a big building opposite the football ground where they used to sell the cattle.

Farmers with a horsebox, and trailers, lorries turning. They'd have to get the pigs into one pen, sows and pigs, baby pigs, ewes and lambs in another . . .

Bromyard's self-styled 'Smithfield' market in 1901 with 876 bullocks for sale. The auctioneers were Ralph Knight.

Ledbury livestock market in the days when it was still held in the streets. (Tilley Collection, Derek Maisey)

I just remember the Market as being enormous, every day of the week, horses, cattle, pigs all sorts of things. Huge market and all the stock would come in from all around. I loved the market, I used to walk to the Market to the stables, just to see the animals. All these cheapjacks. People used to bargain, selling medicines and all sorts.

Everybody knew everybody. I was talking to a lovely girl who used to be in the National Bank in Broad Street one day and she said: 'Do you know, when I was in the bank, you might look through the window and you'd see somebody walking down by the Green Dragon who you didn't know and you'd ask: 'Who is that?' Now you wouldn't know anybody in Hereford.

DRESSED IN THEIR BEST

You would dress up a little bit to go to Market. Course Market was the highlight of the week for the farmers. It was all the entertainment they got. And they used to make a good day of it. It was a chance to socialise and gossip. If they had a good day, a good price for their stock, they'd celebrate a little bit and sometimes wouldn't get home until ten o'clock. Even if they had a bad price they would! That was what the Market was about: a chance to get together.

On a Wednesday Market farmers would have their shoes or boots and gaiters polished. Breeches and leggings. I had hobnailed boots on the farm when I was a student and wore Wellingtons in the winter. And I wore a cotton farm smock over my clothes and an overcoat in the winter. I wore them on Market day — you had to look the part when you went to market.

I went with my father but I don't remember anything except the Market seemed to be a place where you could easily get lost. I used to make sure that I kept with him all the time. My father never went to Market in his working clothes. In those days farmers didn't go to Market every week like they did in later years, because they'd got plenty to do at home. They more or less went once now and again either to see what trade was like or to buy or sell something.

A prize bull in Hereford's new cattle market in the late 1800s with Miss Bulmer's field behind. (Herefordshire Cattle Society)

If you wanted a cooked dinner you could go up town to Lodges, at the back of the Butter Market in Maylord Street. You could have a plate piled up with as much as you could eat. A lot of the dealers and that sort of people went up there.

GINNY LODGE
There was a famous old cattle dealer from Abergavenny. He used to get very very drunk and he often slept in the Market with the cattle. But he'd been successful. He had lots of money although he could hardly read or write. He always wanted somewhere to go for a decent bit of food and he knew this lady, Ginny Lodge, who was a good cook. She was a lovely lady.

So he bought premises at the back of the Butter Market and he put her in there so that he could have a good dinner for him every

Leominster stock market in the 1950s. (Brightwells)

week and serve as many other people as she wanted to. And she got a living Ginny did and everybody was happy.

The Market was a social occasion, husbands, wives came together. The wives went shopping. Wednesday was the busy days but Hereford was more than once a week. We were very busy on other days. There wasn't another Market in the United Kingdom that had a five-day market.

HIVE OF ACTIVITY
Hereford was the biggest turnover of a council-owned market in the country.

It was the largest through-put market. Banbury was a big market, but we did five days a week. We were selling every day of the week.

Fat stock on a Monday: sheep, pigs and cattle for the meat trade. Cattle for the beef trade, sheep for the lamb trade, pigs for the pork trade. That was a Monday. Tuesday it was either horses or pedigree Hereford cattle. Wednesday it was pigs to be furthered on, ewe sales, lamb sales, barren ewe sales, breeding ewe sales, ewes and lambs, whatever the time of year in the sheep business. Rams in the autumn. You also had baby calves and young cattle. Thursday there were store cattle. In the early days these were two-day sales, Thursday and Friday, but they were once a month in those days. Latterly they became weekly. And then you also had the barren cow, which is the end of the dairy beast. And then on Friday was dairy cattle.

I think the best turnover we ever had was about 48 million beasts in a year. It was an amazing business.

Auctioneer Graham Baker with Mr and Mrs Roy Cox of Yarkhill Court, proud owners of the Calf Show Reserve Champion. (Graham Baker)

People used to take young kids to the Market because it was a form of entertainment. In the school holidays people with kids came to see the baby chicks. They loved it. It was a social thing. It was educational.

The market was a real hub of activity and finance. There was a lot of money flowing into town every day. Drovers, people marshalling the animals, people helping the lorries to get loaded at the end of the day, all that sort of business. And of course the auctioneers would employ quite a lot of people.

In the late 1960s the Market was completely rebuilt. Hereford Market was one of the best livestock centres in the United Kingdom.

The Market was run by Hereford Council with a Watch and Markets Committee. Then you had a market superintendent in the market and staff and then all the cleaners and they were run by the council. Auctioneers paid a rent for the service they provided to be able to do the job.

They had their washing down people that were employed by them. Great team. Far too many probably, but a great team. I remember when they had the dustmen's strike (in the 1970s) and they were in the same union and they all went on strike. So we'd carry on and do our sales and then put our waterproofs on and wash the bloody market! Which was great fun for a long time wasn't it? And we had people picketing on the gates trying to stop the livestock coming in. That's how it was.

It changed then. The councils have these things called Central Administration Charges and they stick them on to every one of their departments and of course they put thousands and thousands of pounds on the poor old Market and the Market Committee just couldn't show a profit.

So they came to the auctioneers and said: 'Why don't you run it all?' So we amalgamated the auctioneers, that was Hammonds, Sunderlands, Russell Baldwin and Bright and we called ourselves Hereford Market Auctioneers. And we ran it.

THE HUB OF HEREFORDSHIRE

That way of life's gone. The Market was a centre of the whole rural community. There was a lot of traditions. People came and bought the same people's stock each year. Particularly ewe sales and that. They would come season after season and buy the same person's things. That probably was confidence in the commodity as much as anything.

In the 1950s the Market was mostly male. A farmer's wife may come in if she'd lost her husband and she wanted to sell something, or if her husband was ill and he couldn't get there. They perhaps came more often into the dairy cows' sales on a Friday.

On the Wednesday Market you used to get a lot of people from the Hay-on-Wye area, Kington, Leominster and Bromyard, not so many people from Ross. And a different sort of housewife. The housewives who made butter and kept chickens were different sorts of wives than say the farmers' wives from south-east Herefordshire.

It was a male world. The first lady to start to break in was Peggy Peatt, Alfred Hammond's daughter. I remember saying to Peggy:

'Peggy, you've got to start auctioneering.' 'Not bloody likely!' she said. Because of course they never wore trousers, you'd have these lads with the sticks . . .

Then there were the Miss Watkinses of Turnastone, Vowchurch, Every autumn their Hereford cattle used to come and win the prize. They always came to the October sale with these cattle and they would always go and buy themselves new hats. So they always came in the market in their hats. They were tremendous characters.

The Market used to be the hub of Herefordshire. But things are changing . . . and if they move the market it'll just die.

MEETING THE QUEEN

Terry Court remembered when the Queen came to open the Langford saleroom. It was quite a day for us auctioneers. I was out in the Market introducing the Queen to the porters. There was William Batchstone and Bronco Bushel and Sam Lilly. Sam used to smoke cigarettes without lighting them: he'd suck 'em and they'd get very brown and dirty. Then he'd break them, turn them round and pop the other end in. He never had one out of his mouth. Bronco used to chew tobacco until it had no flavour left in it at all then he would put it in his tin. When it dried he'd smoke it.

And Bailey Nott, our numbering porter, would be covered from head to toe in cow dung and flour and water 'cos we used a mixture of flour and water paste to stick the numbers on the cattle. This particular day we got him fairly smart, he still had a bit of old stuff on his fingers and I said to him: You really ought to go and wash your hands. You don't want to shake the Queen's hand with that!

Anyway the Queen came through the Langford Saleroom and she was already in the gap between lairage and the saleroom before

I could get Bronco to spit out his tobacco and Sam to spit out his cigarette! Then she came in and I introduced her to my team.

When the Queen and the Duke of Edinburgh came to the sale ring where the cattle are sold, we all stood and applauded, recalled Julian Gallimore. The Duke turned round to point out to her that they had just passed over the weighbridge — suddenly we all knew the Queen's weight in hundredweights and quarters.

Staff from Hereford City Survey department await the Queen's visit in 1957. (Ron Chatburn)

Origins of the Market

The origins of Herefordshire Markets date back over twelve centuries.

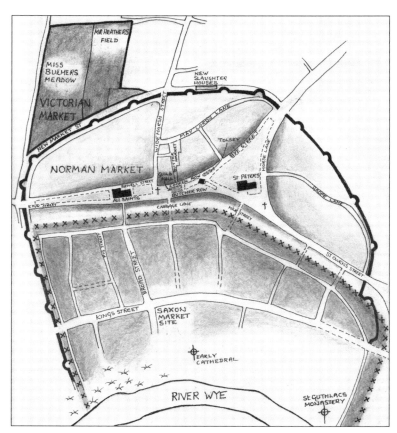

The development of the city's market places from the 8th to the 19th century. (Bobbie Blackwell)

THE SAXON MARKET

Eleven hundred years ago the Saxon king, Edward the Elder (899–924), decreed that all buying and selling must take place in open markets. By the end of the 10th century, Hereford, an important Saxon centre, was holding regular open markets close to the modern Cathedral Close. This was the site of a crossroads, the east to west route linking King Street with Castle Street. The city's main thoroughfare, the road passed in front of Bishop Athelstan's earlier stone cathedral, situated then slightly river-ward of its present position.

THE NORMAN MARKET

After the Norman invasion of 1066 William the Conqueror made his good friend, William FitzOsbern of Normandy, Earl of Hereford, giving him responsibility for the city and the defence of the borderlands between Ludlow and Chepstow. In a deal with the Saxon Bishop Walter, FitzOsbern acquired a large triangular piece of land, stretching from Eign Gate to the bottom of Commercial Street, just north of the Hereford ramparts. The new marketplace and commercial centre for Hereford was created here.

His new market was similar in design to the marketplace of his hometown, Breteuil-sur-Iton, on the southern borders of Normandy and land around the marketplace was set aside to house those of his Norman neighbours who chose to move to Hereford.

All Saints Church was built at the head of Broad Street directly outside what was then the North Gate of the Saxon city, marking the boundary between the old Saxon and new Norman city. Within twenty years of the Conquest, Walter de Lacy had built the church of St Peters, on a spot dominating the eastern aspect of the new marketplace. And so the trading of goods and livestock continued between these two imposing Norman churches, no doubt serving to remind a defeated, disenfranchised and disgruntled Saxon population who their new masters were.

A High Cross was erected where Widemarsh Street entered the new High Town. Similar in appearance to the White Cross, these crosses had a social and religious significance, symbolising the temporal and the spiritual nature of life. The High Cross provided a platform for preachers; an assembly point for lawmakers, an indication of a rightful marketplace, a seat for the weary and, on occasions, a place to display the heads of the beheaded.

In time temporary market stalls gave way to more permanent structures and more permanent trading gave way to homes. Union, Commercial, St Peters, and Eign Gate Streets were established. Over the centuries these streets witnessed the arrival of cattle, pigs, sheep and fowl, drovers, traders, travellers, musicians and entertainers passing through one of the six city gates.

Between 1227 and 1482 a series of Royal Charters were granted to 5,000 towns across the kingdom. These bestowed certain trading privileges on local people who were also empowered to impose and collect taxes. Under its Royal Charter, Hereford was granted three weekly markets and two annual fairs. The fairs took place in the streets during May and October.

Henry I was a wise king who realised that his defeated Saxon subjects would remain hostile to their Norman masters unless they were given some privileges. He granted Hereford a nine-day May fair devoted as much to pleasure as it was to business. (The fair had been reduced to three days by 1854.) The Great October fair was principally for the sale of livestock and agricultural products.

From around the 13th century the administration of the market fell to the Tolsey. This Old French word is derived from *toll*, 'the right of a lord to take payment or commission on the sale of cattle or goods within his estate'. The Tolsey was a stone building that stood in the centre of Commercial Street where it opens into High Town. It was a multifunctional administrative centre dealing with trading, tax and toll collections, the settling of disputes and the enforcement of law and order within the market place.

THE MIDDLE AGES AND BEYOND
By the 16th century half-timbered buildings formed a spine through the centre of High Town, separated from the Old House by a passageway called Golden Alley.

Cooken Row, the street north of this spine, specialised in breads and pastries while Butchers Row to the south was a collection of butchers' shops each with its own abattoir where animals brought to market were slaughtered and sold for meat.

Different streets traded in different commodities. The sale of butter and cheese continued in St Peters Square around another cross, the Low Cross. Garden produce was sold in Cabbage Lane (Church Street). The pig market was in Aubrey Street; cattle and sheep were sold in Broad Street; butter, poultry and ironmongery in High Town, and meat in Bye (later Commercial) Street. Wheat and grain were sold in the old Market Hall (later the site of the Butter Market), while leather, flannel and woollen goods were sold at the Booth Hall. Later, when peace had been established between the Welsh and the English, Welsh traders brought salt, butter and clothing to sell in Hereford.

Hereford's 16th-century Guild Hall showing the city's first public clock. (Drawing by Robert Williams I.F.A. & A.A.I.S.)

Wealthy local merchants built fine city buildings such as the Guild or Market Hall, built in the 1590s on the end of Butchers Row. Twenty-seven pillars supported two splendid floors, the first for the magistrates and assize courts while the top floor housed Hereford's fourteen trade guilds. Between the pillars below, local market traders were able to enjoy some shelter from the elements.

Bells rather than clocks marked time, calling citizens to religious processions and festivals, warning of fire or approaching enemies. And just as it does today in the Cattle Market, a bell marked the opening and closing of street trading. In winter the market bell rang at 9 o'clock in the morning, in summer at 7 o'clock.

When a clock was placed on the new Market Hall the traditional market bell was incorporated into the design with two quarter jacks (youths) adorning each side of the clockface and sounding the quarter hours.

These wooden quarter jacks adorning the Guild Hall clock and struck on the quarter hours

Bells and clocks continued to govern market trading in Hereford and its neighbouring market towns like Ross, Bromyard, Ledbury, Kington and Leominster. Before its demolition the old Corn Exchange in Broad Street (later the Kemble Theatre) supported a magnificent clock tower, and when the Butter Market was built a clock was set over the entrance. In 2007 a hand bell is still rung in the Cattle Market to mark the start of trading.

By the late 17th century Hereford's town centre was overcrowded, congested and filthy. The lack of sanitation triggered repeated epidemics of typhoid, cholera and dysentery. No wonder Daniel Defoe described Hereford as a 'truly old, mean built and very dirty city' when he passed through in 1724. Meanwhile in 1796 one John Price was concerned about the effect on young children of howling animals being slaughtered in the street.

By the 18th century, as the link between poor sanitation and disease was realised, attempts were made to clean up Hereford with the introduction of paving and street lighting and some street widening. Then between 1782 and 1799 Hereford's six medieval gates where demolished so as to let air and light into the city. The High Town's High Cross was pulled down by 1776 along with pillories, stocks and probably the Tolsey. The infamous Butchers Row with its open abattoirs had been demolished by 1837, new slaughterhouses being built out of sight on Blue School Street.

The Guild Hall was pulled down in 1862, the Old House escaping demolition perhaps because by this time it was The George pub. In 1929 it was turned into a museum.

THE FIRST BUTTER MARKET

In 1809 a public meeting was held to consider moving the sprawl of street stalls into one area. In 1810 the site of the old Town Hall was chosen for a butter and poultry market. Extensive improvements were made to the site and in 1860 the market reopened as a covered hall much as it is today while livestock continued to be sold in Broad Street, King Street, Pig (Aubrey) Street and Nicholas Street in all weathers.

Hereford's cattle sales in Broad Street at the turn of the 19th century. (Herefordshire Archive Service)

Broad Street's Market Day in 1880 with the Corn Exchange and its clock tower on the left. The Exchange was later converted into the Kemble Theatre, but demolished in 1963. (Herefordshire Libraries)

An aerial view of Cattle Market in 1953. (Graham Baker)

The Market in 1965. Note the Power Station off centre right and the two open water tanks to the left of it. The tanks were later covered to prevent them being used to drown dogs and dump bikes. (Graham Baker)

An early scene of Hereford Market with the city's electricity generating board's condensing tower in the background. (Hereford Cattle Society)

THE FIRST CATTLE MARKET

In 1844 local auctioneer William James pointed out that, while Hereford had the best provincial livestock market in the region, it had 'the worst accommodation'. By 1853 with the arrival of the railways and with new markets appearing in Leominster, Shrewsbury and Newport, the Hereford Corporation held a meeting in the City Arms Hotel (later Barclays Bank) to establish potential sites for a new Cattle Market. By chance one Mr Heather, who had been responsible for the removal of Butchers

Row, owned and offered a plot of land between Widemarsh Street and Edgar Street to the Corporation on 'fair terms'. Approached by four main roads, the site was close to the city centre and the new railway network.

The land was purchased for £2,500 and a further £4,000 was spent installing drainage, sheds and accommodation pens for sheep, pigs and cattle. New Market Street (previously a narrow track called Brook Side which followed the city ditch) was widened and improved for market access. On 17 October 1856 Hereford's new Cattle Market was officially opened to the public.

By 1888 the council had set its sights on another acre of meadowland adjoining the new market belonging to a Miss Bulmer. When the Corporation approached her with a view to purchase, she did not offer such 'fair terms' as Mr Heather. In order to pay the asking price of £5,000 the council took out a loan from the Treasury, granted on the recommendations of the Inspector of the Government Board.

In 1897, 210 feet of new shedding on the north side of the horse market was added with an enclosed space of 230 feet for a horse run. By 1904 covered pig and calf pens had also been added. Small cattle sales continued in the streets until 1896 when the practice was finally banned.

In 1914 a siding known by the railway men as the Showyard siding was run onto Edgar Street from Barton Yard. Initially this crossed the road into the Market enabling animals to be off-loaded directly on the Market site, and coal to the city's electricity generating station which stood on the Widemarsh Street side of the Market.

WIFE FOR SALE

Along with his cow or pig, a man's possessions once upon a time included his wife. Marriage, formalised in the sixteenth century, became a legal arrangement that enabled the husband to posses not only the wife, but her land and possessions too. Getting divorced required an Act of Parliament.

But within isolated agricultural communities, the poor had little need of formal marriages, having nothing material to gain from it. Local authorities, while they upheld the legalities of a formal marriage, accepted common law customs: and that included selling or exchanging a wife in the Market.

In an 1876 edition of the *Hereford Times* a female correspondent described three occasions in her lifetime when she witnessed the sale of a wife. The first sale was in Aubrey Street, prior to 1810, then the site of the Pig Market. Under the heading 'Wife selling in Hereford in olden times' she wrote:

'Walking across Hereford from Barton to the other side of town with my friend Mona Delnotte Coates we passed the bottom of the Pig Market. Here we saw a crowd and in the centres we saw a woman dressed in a red cloak standing with a very smart hat in her hand. She stood very still looking down and around her neck was a rope and behind her a man was holding the other end of it. Believing she was going to be hung we asked what she had done. A bystander told us: 'Oh she has done no good depend upon it or else he wouldn't want to sell her.'

One man, Jack, offered a shilling for her. Another shouted out: 'Well done Jack. That is eleven pence more than I would give. It's too much boy, too much.'

What am I bid? Women were sold at Hereford Market in the 1800s. (Herefordshire Libraries)

But Jack stood firm.

'I'll take it, though her good looks ort to bring more than that,' said the husband.

'Keep her, keep her for her good looks,' shouted a bystander.

'No,' said another, 'Good looks won't put the vitals on the table without willing hands.'

'Well,' said Jack, 'Here's the shilling and I'll warrant she'll put the vitals on the table and I'll help her get it first.'

Turning to the woman, Jack said: 'Be you willing, missis, to leave him and take me for better or worse?'

'I be willing,' said she.

'And be you willing to sell her for what I bid?' said Jack to the husband.

'I be and will give you the rope into the bargain,' said he.

So Jack walked off up the Pig Market leading his newly-bought wife by the halter. Jack was a weaver by trade and later enquiries revealed this formerly unhappy woman had settled and helped in his business.

Later, wrote the correspondent, another woman was sold in the Butter Market in much the same way. Some years on several more wives were sold in Hereford, despite crying and begging on their bended knees not to be sold. The correspondent recorded that one of these women was never able to forget the humiliation of being sold in public.

The later sales occurred after 1810 when the new Butter Market was built. The practice of wife selling in the marketplace was not confined to Hereford. Market tolls record the sale of wives at Birmingham in 1773, Sheffield in 1796 and Brighton in 1826.

Bobbie Blackwell

Auctioneers

What am I bid? For the fast talking auctioneer, the Market was both a challenge and a pleasure.

YOU NAME IT. WE'VE SOLD IT

There was more to auctioning than getting up and shouting and waving a gavel about. That was the easy part to be honest with you.

You couldn't bribe the auctioneer. Whatever he said, it went and that was it. Once the hammer went down, that's it. If there was any dispute, they'd bring 'em back and sell 'em again. If one said: 'Oh, I didn't bid on that,' then: 'Bring it back and we'll sell it again.'

Auctioneering is really only a sophisticated form of counting. You got to be able to count: you need to be able to go: 'One, two, three' — that helps, obviously. You need to know a bit about selling. And you need to be a bit of a show-off.

But it doesn't actually matter because if you changed your style a bit on various things, you could sell anything. You name it, I bet we've sold it at one time in our lives. Tanks, hairbrushes, furniture, pedigree cattle, pedigree horses, pedigree sheep, commercial sheep, commercial cattle, farm implements, farms, land, houses, garden equipment, tools, cars, 4x4s, furniture, lorries. One day we sold 2.4 million traffic cones! We grew up selling anything.

I'm always amazed when people look at jewellery and know what it's worth. But it's the same with cattle. When cattle tended to be sold by the hundredweight, you'd go for the size and the weight and convert it. So you would tend to say: 'The bullocks today are worth £10 or £12 to a hundredweight so if that's five, five and half hundredweight, well that's sixty pounds.' Obviously, the better ones might make £12 and the others might make the £10. You're not going to be that far out.

It is a different way of life being a livestock auctioneer. Until a man sells for the first time you don't really know whether he's going to make it. There was an auctioneer with a terrible stutter . . . until he got up to sell. You just don't know until he starts selling. Livestock auctioneers can probably sell anything if they get enough practice, although you can't make a fine art auctioneer into a livestock auctioneer.

WALKING THE PLANK

They wouldn't allow you to get up and do it straight. Three years apprenticeship it was as a pupil in the auctioneers company.

My father was a tailor and outfitter in Hereford, recalled *Colin Manning*. I'd been at the Cathedral School and, as National Service was being done and I was finishing in the autumn of 1944, I had the chance to join the Fleet Air Arm, which I did. But I had to wait three months and I met Cyril Duffield of Sunderlands one day and he said: 'Well, he'd better come to the market and work for me for a month.' I went for a month and stayed fifty years.

The older generation — Alfred Hammond, Cyril Duffield, Frank Russell, Jack Lyke — were looking for younger people. So at the age of 17½, I had the chance to sell the calves for the first time. It was sudden death: you were on the plank, Alfred Hammond suddenly passed you the stick and said: 'Here you are Manning, you better get on with this.'

For my first venture into selling, *Graham Baker* recalled, I was stood by my boss, Danny Clifton, while he was selling away. Then he said: 'Right Graham, come on. Your turn.' He handed me the gavel. I was dumbstruck for about five minutes, but what he had done, of course, was prompted the buyers that they were to bid, to help me on my first day.

Auctioneers Bill Gallimore and Jack Lyke. (Julian Gallimore)

The Market wasn't covered in those days and you would walk 'the plank'. If it was very cold, the plank would be icy. You'd need to walk carefully. The cattle people bid by flicking the finger or just an intonation or a nod. You wouldn't notice who's bidding unless you looked carefully. A lot of bidding was done by tapping your leg with a stick or pinching your leg. And if you missed a bid they'd remind you. You'd have glasses taken off and: 'Would you like these?' You'd have your leg pulled in no uncertain terms.

Different people bid in different ways. Some blinked an eye, others waved their hand. Everyone was trying to be discreet, trying to bid, but not be noticed by other buyers in case their competition is too great.

In the school holidays they gave me a job for 5/- to come and run the slips. The clerk to the auctioneer would note down how much the beasts made and the name of the purchaser. When he finished a pad of sheets with about five lots they'd tear those off the pad and we'd take that sales slip from the ring, or the auctioneer if he's on the plank in the sheep market, to the office so they could record then.

MIME ARTIST
When the animals came out of the ring they were marked for the particular buyer: they might cut the hair off the bottom of their tail, or put a scissors mark up on the flank. Then he'd shout to the chap at the far end of the alley: 'This is so and so's beast'.

There was one firm, Cheltenham Butchers, and another called Evans Campion and Blakemore from Wolverhampton.

One buyer, Bunter Fletcher from Leominster, had lost his voice. So for Evans, Campion and Blakemore from Wolverhampton he used to pretend to kick a football (Wolverhampton Wanderers) and for Cheltenham Butchers he used to make a sign as if he was drinking a pint of beer because of the old Cheltenham and Hereford brewery.

The cattle used to be transported away to a great extent by rail. And the trains actually came into Hereford market. If you go down Edgar Street today, the railway used to come across the road there,

Mr Hammond the auctioneer, third from the right, would acknowledge a bidder with 'you with the wart on your nose' or 'you with the big ears.' (Sunderlands)

where the Salvation Army Citadel is. Trains came in there, and one of my first jobs was to ensure there was enough cattle wagons ready for the cattle through Great Western Railways — contacting them and arranging for the trucks to come into the Market and they'd be loaded then and sent on their way.

We used to have a chap called Charlie Anderson who regularly came from Scotland, and a man called Duggins who came from Astwood Bank, Droitwich, but he would fly back and forth from Aberdeen, in the days when flying was hardly heard of. They were commission men, they would buy for large firms. Baxters would have a buyer regularly at Hereford, Bill Tingle, who would come and stand in his one place. If anybody stood there, they were moved over. Later there were several people buying for halal.

Hammond and Penry Jones joined with Sunderlands to make it Sunderlands and Hammond. Then we were Russell, Baldwin and Bright and then it was Sunderlands Hammond. Penry Jones worked for Hammonds and the pigs were done by them. Then the cattle, sheep, calves and everything were done alternative weeks by us so we would sell sheep one week and cattle the next week and Sunderlands would sell sheep one week and cattle the next and Sunderlands would do the calf sales.

The auctioneers oiled the works a bit: we facilitated things by doing quite a bit of money lending to farmers based on the fact that if you bring your stock back to us to sell, we'll help you out over a period of time. There were always bad debts.

On the plank. Auctioneers Chris Voyce and Michael Evans at Hereford Market.

THE LOUDEST AUCTIONEER

David Probert received a letter from the Health and Safety Executive in Worcester.

They said they understood that my voice was so loud when I was selling chickens that it could indeed be a danger to human health and hearing. If it had been April 1st I would have definitely thought that this is a really good joke.

Apparently somebody complained about my voice. Several weeks before this happened, a guy who was not a regular market trader pulled his van up outside the doors of my chicken shed, so that you couldn't get in there. I asked him to move. And he refused. So I parked my car so tight against his table, that he couldn't sell anything. He was very upset with me. I've not seen him since, and it may not be him, but I can only guess.

80 decibels apparently sounds like a radio playing very loud inside a tractor cab with the engine running. 120 decibels, what does that sound like? 120 decibels is equivalent to standing within 30 metres of a jet aircraft taking off. Bloody hell, I thought. I'm bloody loud.

They started to threaten proceedings so I rang: 'I do not sound like a jet aircraft taking off. I'm just going to ignore you because you're just being so damn stupid.'

They sent me a letter again: 'You must respond otherwise action will be taken and you do realise that we have the power to close your business down.' I went to the press. It came out in the *Hereford Times* and all hell was let loose. I had every single major broadsheet and tabloid paper in the country ringing me up. I got Jeremy Vine from Radio 2 and a driveway full of TV vans. It was extraordinary. But we never heard from the Health and Safety Executive again. Public time and money. It was a total, total nonsense.

The Cattle Market

In the new millennium dairy farming is in decline. But the cattle trade was once central to the business of Hereford Market.

THOUSANDS OF CATTLE

Hereford was predominantly a cattle centre. The cattle came to Hereford from all round. All the market towns in Herefordshire — Ledbury, Bromyard, Ross, Leominster — are one day's cattle walk, fourteen, fifteen miles, away from the Hereford Market.

At one stage there were thousands of cattle. A fat market on a Monday, normal traditional Wednesday market, store cattle on a Thursday with an average of a thousand cattle plus, and on the big sales two thousand a day. On Friday it would be the sale of the female cattle, the heifers, and there was a dairy sale every Friday with a hundred, hundred and fifty cattle. And then on a Saturday, there were the horse sales. There were sales of everything basically going on. Of course there were thousands of smallholdings whereas now there's only really a handful left. All that has changed. Now Hereford is more essentially a sheep centre because the number of cattle have declined.

At one stage there would be two solid days of selling store cattle. There would be one day on a Thursday which would be for bullocks, for steers only, and then on the Friday there would be heifers only. There were so many cattle, the whole Market would be full. I suppose it could have held 2,000 to 2,500 store cattle, and that was every week, not once a month as it is now with about 30 there. How times have changed!

RECYCLING

The number of store cattle was extraordinary. Because we had the flow with all those calves that came there. They were fed up and brought on to be young store beasts ready to go for fattening. In those days farming was fairly old fashioned and so the pattern was in broad terms, calves into Hereford Market from the dairy herds, then out to the rearing fields of the borders. They would be reared and fed on the grass up there until they were twelve, eighteen months old, then back into Hereford market to be sold to go fattening.

You'd get the guys coming from the eastern counties, the fattening guys, who were growing cereals and wanted to put cattle into the sheds to feed them, to use the straw up they'd got, so the straw would go back out and have the continuous cycle of re-energising the ground with the farmyard manure. It was all recycling really.

All that has kind of faded into the past.

On a Thursday, when they were selling all these cattle, the big auction room which used to be called the Langford Sale Ring would be heaving, packed, every single seat taken and people standing. It was a really busy sale. These dealers, they were wonderful characters.

A cattle dealer was someone who bought animals in one market and then either sold them to customers, or resold them in another Cattle Market.

We were second to Smithfield in those days. Alderman Powell, he had the Christmas Fat Stock show and there were the most magnificent trophies for those cattle prizes and everything.

Dairy cattle

Father had a good time in his life, *John Matthews* recalled. He was a Bristol policeman, he'd been a bomber pilot in the war. He survived. So when he came back, he settled into a bit of farming. He was a farmer through and through. Loved his cattle. We'd always had a lot of cows. Mostly Friesian cows now. At the Market he would buy cows. At the start he kept what he called a flying herd. In other words, he'd buy his cattle from the Market on a Friday, fresh calved so they were full of milk. We only had room at Bartonsham then for about 80 cows, and initially we milked them all by hand! When I was a little boy! Dad had half a dozen people sit on milking stools at six o clock in the morning, milk these cows, men principally. Then they'd clean them all out, they'd be tied by a chain round the neck, they didn't go out at all in winter. They were cosseted these cows! They'd calve once a year, well you had to have a calf or else you wouldn't get any milk! For one period they're dry, in other words not giving any milk, building up their reserves for their calf. So they're dry for about three or four weeks, perhaps six weeks, then they're milking again. But we wouldn't have any like that, we'd just milk these cows and sell 'em for meat.

You'd just milk 'em and sell 'em at the market. So we didn't have any animals around that were non-producers.

But, like all things change, that system fell apart. Fresh calved cows were sold on a Friday in the Market and there wasn't enough cows to buy every Friday. You'd have over 100, perhaps 150 there. And there were lots more dairy farmers, lots of small dairy farmers: everybody had a few cows. Then there were the dealers coming from other parts of the country to buy cows. So you'd get people from Shropshire, Gloucestershire, Somerset. Very busy, the Market.

Everybody knew each other. So you had this system when the buyers and sellers knew each other intimately really. Extraordinary busy and the auctioneers had a critical part to play, definitely.

The Milkers

What you didn't do when you bought your cow to Market to sell her, you didn't milk her the day you brought her so the buyer could see if she was what we call 'even'. You know, there was 'even' milk in every quarter. She was not three quarters. And she didn't have mastitis. Still a problem now, I mean nothing changes. Course they kept 'em in the Market there and the people who were selling 'em, they'd have the soapsuds on 'em and they'd be brushing their tail out! Really good fun! Tremendous.

The Market was all right but I'd always rather be at home. You'd go after you'd done all your work at home and they'd start selling cows about 11 or 12 o'clock, and you'd probably be there an hour before so that you could pick out your cows that you wanted to buy.

You would meet a lot of people. There was the café, which you would go in when you could find the time and get something to eat and a cup of tea.

You'd see perhaps 150 cows, all lined up, all tied up by the neck in the market, with a lot number on 'em. And the person who was selling them might have three or four to sell. Then you'd go and you'd put your hand on her and try her round, you know, draw milk from every quarter to make sure the milk was all right and she didn't have what we call a blind quarter when there's one with nothing in it, 'cause then she's only worth three quarters! The thing is if you've got a three quarters cow, obviously you've lost 25% of the viability. Not so productive and possibly likely to lose an udder. Perhaps she's got mastitis in that one. And of course you gotta check they're quiet because if they kick it's a bit of a headache! And cows do kick very hard, I can tell you. Some cows don't like being milked. And the other thing was, when you were hand-milking them particularly, some cows are very hard to milk. In other words, the teat canal was very small. Oh, it used to make your hands ache! I did a bit of hand-milking. And if you're milking them with a machine, it'd take ages. Sitting on this cow for twenty minutes — no good at all! You want a nice free milker, you want a nice even udder, it's nicely displayed, not out of all proportion, if you've got one udder that's very big, it'll only get worse. It becomes a real nuisance. Then you're looking for a good bodied animal as well. Nice temperament — very important. You get cows that are extremely flighty.

I didn't mind milking by hand. Especially in the winter 'cause it was warm. Got kicked a few times, kicked the bucket over and all. When we'd milked we put the milk in a churn, then you'd usually strain them wouldn't you. Put it through a strainer; get the dirt out, the bits out. Then you would cool it. Well it would be like blood heat wouldn't it? I have drunk it straight from the cow, but I don't know that I was that keen on it. Creamy? It all depends on the cow.

I'd rather work with animals.

And then the machines came in. That was the best things that ever happened when the machines came in. 'Cause one man could do it then, couldn't they?

'You gotta check your cow will draw on all quarters.'
(Graham Baker)

33

Penry Jones (left) was a pig auctioneer but also sold sheep. Here he is with Charlie Miles in 1967 with his Best Sheep trophies.
(Graham Baker)

THE AUCTIONEER

When you're auctioneering over 2,000 store cattle on a two day sale it was bloody hard work. Well you can imagine: you'd have a store cattle sale that went on from half past ten in the morning to six o'clock at night, and then we'd have to assist these guys to mark them all up and put them in their right pens.

You'd put them all in their various lots and then pen them ready in the railway sidings with those great big wooden corrals. Then the train came up to the siding, they'd open the doors and off they'd go . . . Northampton, Essex, Surrey wherever it was.

THE DEALER

My speciality job was dairy cows on a Friday. A customer would come along and say: 'So-and-so's having a sale and I can't go. Buy me a heifer.' Or: 'Buy me a cow.' I'd go and bid for it and take it home. My neighbour, he went out of the dairy cows, and I brought fifty of them into Hereford, anyhow. And sold 'em as they calved. Then we bought Friesian heifers when they were twelve to eighteen months old and took 'em home, got 'em in calf and calved 'em down. I was the first man in here to sell a dairy cow for a thousand pounds. It weren't mine, it was for somebody else. They was just getting up to nine hundred pounds and this chappie said: 'Oh, I can give a thousand pounds' and I said to the auctioneer: 'I got a man here who can give a thousand pounds.' And he said 'we'd better get cracking and see what we can do!' We had one man who came regularly from Cheltenham to buy store cattle. He was obviously a very wealthy man. One day the telephone went and his grandson was on the phone and he said: 'I'm so-and-so's grandson. Granddad's died. He's being cremated on Friday, but he was a loner and we don't think there'll be many people. Would you come?'

I took a lorry driver, Jones from Ludlow, and Michael Duffield and we went to Cheltenham Crematorium. There were only fifteen or eighteen people there. When it came to the end, they played *And the Saints Come Marching In*. Jazz! After the funeral the grandson said: 'That was Granddad playing the clarinet.' He said week in and week out, he drove to Birmingham or to London and played in Ronnie Scott's jazz band. Now this was a man of considerable wealth who was well into his eighties, but he went once a week and played!

THE DAIRY

Edward Matthews was from Hereford originally and he started Bartonsham Dairies. He went to America in 1833, drove a steam train between Chicago and New York, and then came home when the Civil War began. Not many people left America at that time, but he did! He became an engineer here, driving a railway engine between Cardiff and Shrewsbury or Cardiff and Liverpool. But he was injured, getting hit on the head, when driving his train down towards Kilpeck. He became a very religious man then. When he came out of hospital, he couldn't go back on the railway so he bought a cow, rented a bit of land up at Whitecross and started pushing milk down Whitecross Road in a wheelbarrow.

1869, what do you think a cow was worth then? His first cow was Old Brownie. A dairy cow these days is probably worth £800 –£1,000, £1,500 if she's good, but at that time, his first cows were £14 12s 6d, which was a serious lot of money. It was the sort of economy where your value was counted by your cows.

He passed it onto his son who ran the business until 1948. He'd moved from Whitecross. The cows had moved to Westfields then. First of all, he moved to the back of the Booth Hall where they had a milk shop (that's where my father was born).

Then in the early twenties, grandfather took the tenancy of Bartonsham Farm, which was just a little 120-acre farm then, just by the bend of the river. It was a church farm and he got the tenancy off the Church Commissioners.

He went on running the business until he had a stroke. Drank a lot of whiskey and smoked fairly heavily! He was 62, everyone

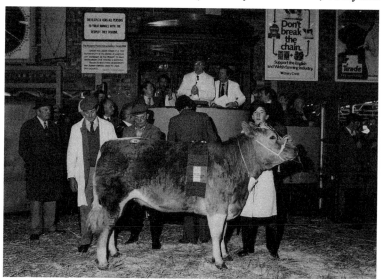

A Christmas Fatstock Show in 1987 with, left, Mr Pritchard, a St Owens Street butcher, Bill Phillips and his son Colin. (Graham Baker)

thought he was going to die overnight. He died when he was 93 in the end!

Father had left the farm to become a policeman in Bristol but he took it on when his father had a stroke. There was four or five little milk cows and some jolly old cows which were milked by hand on Bartonsham Farm. So they'd milk the cows and bring the milk there.

Every Friday my father would go to Market and buy a few cows. Every Thursday he'd sell a few fat cows, and that's the way we went on. He milked about 70 or 80 cows there.

He used the Market to buy and sell cows. So Hereford Market was the key to the whole thing.

THE MILKMAN

I went for an interview with Matthews of Bartonsham, recalled *Tom Wheatstone*. I went there when I was fifteen. Horse and cart days. I first delivered down Park Street with a sandy coloured horse called Mary. She was very frisky! After twelve months, I got taken on another round which was Harold Street and Whitecross. I had a big black horse called Lady, real strong.

I had Lady for seven, eight, years. And then I was moved onto another round with a van and the horses were being replaced. None going now. I hadn't seen Lady for eighteen months. Mr Matthews had put her out to graze before he would sell her, out at a farm at Eaton Bishop, the Marsh Farm, and I went out there one day, to where she was, and I stood on top of the gate and just shouted 'Lady', and she came all the way back up, as if it was yesterday.

Mrs Davis had had the newsagent shop in Edgar Street. She lived in Moorfield Street, and I had a key, to put the milk in the fridge for her. She always left some sugar, which was for the horse. Mrs Davis died one day and there was no more sugar. I went on by without giving the horse any sugar and the horse took a lump out of my shoulder! After that, I used to take sugar with me! I used to give it to her when we got there.

DIED ON THE SCALES

There was an old fellow called Ted Phipps I remember. He used to make sure he got himself into jail for the very coldest months of the year, because that was the warmest place to be. He had nowhere to live. He had nowhere to live so he'd be drunk and disorderly somewhere and he'd get himself slung in the cells for a few weeks. He was estranged from his wife and he was supposed to be paying part of his unemployment allowance to his wife or something, and of course he would make sure that he didn't pay it. They'd come chasing for that as well so he'd get locked up. Very, very unfortunate end poor old Phipps had, because in the Cattle Market there was a very large scales they used to weigh the store cattle at the back of the Langford Sale Ring. Before a cattle sale on a Thursday, and after the calves on a Wednesday, we used to straw it up ready to go and there would be a lot of deep straw on the scales and he used to sleep there and one very cold morning when he hadn't managed to get himself into prison he was found dead on the scales. He'd died in the night and he was practically frozen to the metal which was quite unfortunate.

Pedigree Herefords

The journey of the white-faced Hereford steer from a Herefordshire farmyard in 1720 to world dominance in the beef market is an extraordinary tale. Hereford Market played a unique role in the story.

THE HEREFORDS

The highlight of the Market were the January Bull Sales. Normally a Monday and a Tuesday. The show would be on the Monday and the sale on the Tuesday. People came from all over the world, Argentina and Paraguay, Uruguay and Chile, the Australians, South Africans. These South American ranches, *estancias*, would be there paying vast amounts for these bulls compared to nowadays. There was a huge ball on the Monday night in the Green Dragon.

Bill Gallimore sold Herefords right through the 1950s, 1960s and 1970s. They had a good business, they were the auctioneers to the Society. The Hereford Cattle Society appointed their own auctioneers and they would run pedigree Hereford auctions all over the place. When the spring or autumn sale was on at Hereford Market, my word there were some toffs in town! The Green Dragon was full of them!

During the January Bull Sale there was a taxi man called Len Oliver and he did nothing else for a week before the sale and nothing else after the sale but taxi South Americans from and to London airport.

People would come from all over the United Kingdom to buy at the Hereford Market. Western Masterpiece made 12,500 guineas in 1947. Many a bull sold at 6 or 7,000 quid at the January bull show. And they'd average 400, 500 a piece: oh the South American trade! That's how they started, they'd come over here and buy these good bulls from the Vern and Captain de Quincey and Lewis the Haven.

In 1960 twenty-three bulls went to South America. You'd be pleased to send one now. In those days with the Hereford cattle we were selling between 150 and 500 animals and that Market was absolutely chock bang full of Hereford bulls. Those early days were some real glory days.

The Hereford was generally very docile, very placid. Modern cattle are harder to handle. Someone did take a bull into Rutters the china shop as a publicity stunt.

If a Hereford bull got upset you wondered why. I did remember one, but we came to the conclusion that it must have got upset in the lorry. You never, ever trust a bull, but to see these men working on these Herefords, the bull just standing there chewing the cud as happy as Larry as it's washed with a hose pipe.

The cattle sales were world famous. *Joanne Probert* remembered her father going to Smithfield. He bought the prize Hereford beast for the butchers and it was called Clive Ivy and he made a poem up about it. It was brought to Hereford Station and it came up with all its ribbons and what have you and a whole retinue of people following it.

I'm Clive Ivy don't you know
I won first prize at Smithfield Show
And should you want a real good feed
You can't beat the good old Hereford breed.

They printed it in the *Hereford Times*.

And it stood in one of the loose boxes this beast did, in Edgar Street, and of course all the farmers were popping across from the Market to have a look at it.

The highlight of the market was the sale of pedigree Hereford bulls, seen here in the 1950s with Bill Gallimore as auctioneer. (Julian Gallimore)

In 1928 George Lanman, who was born in Peterchurch, walked this bull to Tenbury Market from Redwood Farm, Middleton on the Hill. (George Lanman)

A pretty prize bull standing on the as yet undeveloped Miss Bulmer's Meadow with the Richmond buildings behind.
(Hereford Cattle Society)

WHITE FACES

The Hereford is a breed that came into being in this county. A group of farmers on the borders of Herefordshire, Shropshire and Wales started to produce this breed and kept breeding and other records.

In 1846 the first breed Herdbook was produced. This continued to be maintained privately until 1878. Then the Hereford Herdbook Society was formed and took on the role of administering the breed all over this country. The Society has been in the same building in Offa Street, Hereford since 1878 and the aims of the Society remain the same as when it was started.

When the first Herdbook was produced in 1846, they entered the cattle that met a criteria that was set by the then breeders. Around 1880, the Herdbook was closed, meaning that every animal then that entered the Herdbook, its parents also had to be in the Herdbook. And that has been maintained ever since. As well as the Hereford Society of the UK, there's another twenty or twenty-five Societies all over the world, and any other Herefords registered by those Societies can all be tracked back through to the original cattle here. The people that breed Hereford cattle pay to register their cattle with us and we produce all the documentation on those cattle for them.

The offices of Hereford Herd Book Society (on the right) in Offa Street, Hereford.

The Hereford is a beef breed and it has a role to play with bulls of the breed going into dairy herds, producing what is known as the Black Hereford. The male calves of that cross will go for beef, the females will normally go forward as what is known as suckler cows, breeding females for the hill farms in Wales, Scotland and the South West, then using another bull onto them to produce beef cattle. But it is a beef breed. The breed has the ability to thrive wherever it goes. It can stand the hot climates of Africa, Australia, South America, or cold climates like Norway, Finland, America and Canada where they can experience temperatures of minus 40. It's a breed that is easy to manage, easy to calve, easy to feed, with high quality meat.

What the breed does have which no other breed has got — the description of the breed if you like — is it's a red-bodied animal with white markings and a white face. The white face is a trademark of the breed. Because if you use a Hereford bull on any other breed, you will always get a white face.

We used to hold five sales a year at the Market, selling up to a thousand cattle, maybe more, in a year. We've had Miss World to open the sale! Then in 1990 the problems with BSE closed the export market, there has been a reduction in breed numbers and more recently the unfortunate incidence of Foot and Mouth. In 2006 there were two sales that moved maybe three hundred cattle.

David Prothero, secretary of the Hereford Cattle Society

A lot of Hereford breeders used W.H. Bustin. When Bustin arrived to take a photograph it was a day's work. He'd very often frighten the hell out of the bulls. He'd have his tripod and he'd get his head in underneath the blanket. Then something wouldn't be quite right: he'd fling the blanket in the air, frighten the bull and have to start all over again.

GOOD BREEDING

When you came to sell it was rather like getting rid of a bit of old jewellery. You became very fond of your cattle and, in a way, it was a very intimate business. You used to take the animals in for the Bull Sales the night before, or early morning of the judging day.

(Hereford Cattle Society)

They'd be all in their rows. People would be there early, before the judging, studying the bulls, then seeing them paraded. A lot of the judging was done before they came in front of the judge.

The last thing the buyer would do is let you know if they were interested in your bull. You mustn't declare your hand, but you might see them coming back with a friend a bit later to have another look.

When you were buying you studied the breeding past of the females and the sire in the hope of producing what you wanted. One never knows quite what child the wife is going to produce. And it's the same with cattle — it all depends on the concentration of blood-lines in your sire.

(Hereford Cattle Society)

And when you bought a bull you could never be sure whether it was going to 'nick' with your females. There was always that element of doubt, but the great breeders could see beyond that fog. And even if everything worked out things could still go wrong at home. The best sire we'd ever had slipped on a concrete causeway and dislocated his hips. We could never use him again and it was a big financial loss.

One Hereford bull sold for sixty thousand, a lot of money in those days, but Hereford prices were never quite as high as the Shorthorns and certainly not as high as the Angus.

LONG DISTANCE DELIVERY

One Herefordshire farmer delivered a Hereford bull to Australia by sea. I got a job on board ship and looked after cattle. There was a Hereford bull, a Devon bull, a Shorthorn, three Suffolk ram lambs, four or five canaries and one Jersey heifer that had just calved. She was in milk and I had strict instructions to dry her off which I paid no attention to because at sea on a cargo boat fresh milk is worth a lot of money. I didn't sell the milk for money: I just swapped it with the officers for better accommodation. Instead of being down in a shabby little hovel in the stern of the ship I ended up having a state room and a steward to look after me and I milked that heifer from Tilbury to Brisbane.

This was the bill for the luncheon that preceded the Griffiths sale of Hereford pedigrees at Alders End, Tarrington in 1920. The first cow sold for almost a thousand guineas and a later lot was sold to the agent of King George V.

The Sheep Market

We did have five sheep escape in the Market. They found their way into Tesco. They didn't go by the right route: they should have gone to the butcher first.

In the 1940s there was a lot more cattle. The sheep section has improved because they're still coming out of North Herefordshire and they're coming this way. There's been one or two very large sheep dealers in Hereford who've been a godsend.

A prize pen of Clun ewes. They belonged to Mr Miles who insisted on being called 'The Master' seen here with his son, the judge Howard Bevan (left), and auctioneer Colin Manning with the certificate. (Graham Baker)

Dad was a sheep and cattle dealer, recalls *Nigel Bowen*. He wanted me to deal. Me older brother didn't like dealing, but I loved it. I skipped school at fourteen, used to ride horses, go hunting, go and buy cattle. First two black bullocks I bought at a farm sale I sold in Hereford Market and I got £25 so I never went to school again. I'd been going to the Market with my Dad since I was about 8. Used to wear trousers, jumper and shirt. You wouldn't go scruffy would you? Your dad would kick your backside! He always had clean shoes, and a jacket and tie and a trilby hat.

Dad gave me a couple of Jacobs when I was a kid. From 14 I started sheep farming. My dad was going on holiday and he said 'You sell the sheep for the best you can' and that was that. I was selling 100, 200 ewes, all two year olds. I had to stand in the box by the auctioneer. If you didn't get enough you'd bring them home, but nine times out of ten, good trade or bad, you sold them. Dad was brilliant to me. If you bought something too dear: 'You go and sell it, boy'. You soon learned.

You used to sell tups by the old metal railings by the Market Tavern on a Wednesday. My dad would be buying store lambs and I would be buying the tups, whatever was old enough for killing. That was when I was 15 or 16.

By the cow pens there used to be two rings and there used to be conker trees there. We used to get the conkers as kids. You'd be there all day, go to the Dean Leigh for lunch — a pork pie was a shilling. Dad didn't go to the pubs: business is day time, drinking is night time.

I'm a sheep and beef cattle farmer now. Things might have changed, but the prices haven't!

The sheep numbers, they're nothing like they used to be in Hereford Market. On a good day there, when there was a combination of store lambs, breeding rams, cull ewes, breeding ewes — they were separate, special sales on Saturdays — the whole place would be overflowing. I would say 6,000 to 8,000 sheep in there on a Wednesday. The success of the place was adding

Famous drover Freddie Fox at the Sheep sales in the 1950s.
(Graham Baker)

to its own downfall, because the traffic problems were horrendous. There were endless rows about where the livestock carriers' lorries could park. You'd get the big dealers coming in from a long way off and they couldn't park and you'd think: 'Oh my god, I can't chuck him out of the Market, because he's going to be one of my main customers'.

I just love sheep and cattle. Don't know why.

When I was a kid you could sell sheep all afternoon. People came from all over. There's none of this dealing like there used to be: six-day rule, passports, movements, Foot and Mouth; it's all changed.

(Bobbie Blackwell)

The Pig Market

I first started going to Hereford Market with some pigs at the end of the 1940s. The pig market was run by Hammond and Co in those days on a Wednesday. I would take a belly of pigs, which was a litter, maybe eight or ten or twelve if the sow had had a lot.

On a Wednesday Market Day I'd get up about 5 or 6 o'clock. Used to get to market in a horse and trap from Tillington with my father and grandfather or go with Mr Breeze from Wormsley with his horse and float. A float was more of a working cart, a two-wheeler, one axle, open cart. Used to put the pigs in and throw a net over the top and I'd be sitting on the side above the wheel. Old Mr Breeze, he'd be at the front there with his whip and his wife, or maybe his daughter. He was a character. He lived on Hill Farm at the top of Wormsley and he was one of the last people to wear breeches to Market. A proper farmer.

Took us about half an hour. There'd be a line of horse and carts at Whitecross, maybe the odd tractor. We'd leave the horse at the Horse and Groom pub, which was by the Eye Hospital, and stable it up there. Horse and Groom had a big yard as well as stables, so the horse could go outside if there was no stables left for us. We would drop the pigs off at the Market — one of us would stay with the pigs, the auctioneer and all of that rigmarole — and somebody else would take the horse and trap back to stables, unhitch the horse. There was a fee.

Though it was quite a way from the Market, the Horse and Groom was a busy pub. We would go to the Dean Leigh in the middle of the day and back to the Horse and Groom at the end.

The auctioneers always sold the pigs first and all the farmers used to come into the pig Market to take a look at the trade and have a chat.

It would be quite a throng in there. And then they'd start selling. One auctioneer, Penry Jones, would ask for a price for this pen of weaners. One of the buyers would point and ask: 'What about that little one there?' as if he'd asked too much. 'Well,' Penry would say, he was a great big fella, 'I was a little one once!'

One time Graham Baker was selling. He looked at this sheet and said: 'I've got two gilts here running with the boar — it doesn't say whether they were running towards him or running away from him'!

Once a schoolteacher came in the Market with a class of school children. They all had their boards and they were writing things, and she was pointing to the pigs and talking to the children. Meanwhile a butcher or a dealer was buying the pigs, and Graham Baker banged the hammer and said: 'Sold to the lady in glasses and the red jumper.'

She was aghast for a minute or two. He said: 'Name madam, please?' And just when she was going to collapse he said: 'Sold to the dealer'. It was all in good fun. I suppose if you got the buyers in a good mood then perhaps they would bid better.

That was a big thing on a Wednesday; lots of things to walk round. When I was small I used to keep pretty close to father at Market. At the fall of the hammer you paid at the office. But the pig market was very good because you could go for your money, a cheque or cash, on the same day. And there were sub-branches of all the banks at Market so you could walk straight into your bank and put the money in. Very often it was desperately needed. So it has changed tremendously.

Jim Pritchard who owned the slaughterhouse used to kill 74 pigs on a Monday morning and they would be on the train in Withington at four o'clock in the afternoon.

PIG IN A TREE

In about 1952 I suspect, it was an extremely busy pig market — a huge number of store pigs were sold through there and my father, as a fairly small-time farmer, had pigs as one of his enterprises. In order to secure a pen at a decent place in the auction you had to leave home at about 5 o'clock in the morning. The transport that

we had was very limited and we could only take a few pigs at a time. So I used to load up the first lot and deposit them scattered out amongst a number of pens in the Market in the dark and cold and gloom. I had to make absolutely sure that those pens were reserved until my father got back with the next load because it was extraordinarily busy in the pig section then.

In terms of pigs the Market served pretty much the whole of the county and a lot of South Wales and the Welsh Borders and Worcestershire as well, as those satellite markets along the borders because didn't have the facilities for handling pigs.

You need a different sort of penning because of the way the beasties are. It's not very handy having pigs in large pens with

Up until 1956 the pig pens lined Newmarket Street, seen here with The Market Tavern in the background. (Sunderlands)

The pig pens showing the planks on which auctioneers walked while selling. Peggy Peatt, daughter of auctioneer Alfred E Hammond is on the right. (Sunderlands)

railings that far apart. They'd be off! In the pig market, there was a series of concrete pens the size of a large dining table, where you'd just get a sow and pigs in. They were solid sided and they had close-barred gates on the front. It was all on a very much different scale to the cattle and sheep pens.

In 1972 as auctioneer I sold a hundred and two thousand pigs in the Market in one year. Thirty-five years later I sold about a hundred a fortnight.

Everybody kept pigs in those days. You had a pig bucket in the house and your potato peelings went in, your carrots and a bit of waste milk that went in and you could fatten one or two pigs a

A sale of bacon pigs in 2006 with (left to right) Mr Bowen of Abergavenny, Bill Hyde of Shropshire, Paul Batt of Gloucester and auctioneer Graham Baker. (Graham Baker)

In the mid 1950s Les Jones (left) of Summers Pork Butchers, Ledbury kept an abattoir behind his shop. He killed and dressed up to 200 pigs a week. Bill Summers (centre) and Doug Kington (right) a butcher from the London Central next door are scalding a pig before scraping off the coarse bristles. (Mr and Mrs Les Jones)

year with that. And it would keep you through the winter time. Lovely. Home cured bacon hanging up on the ceiling there in the kitchen above the Aga.

I remember my father once stringing a great big pig up on a tree outside the cellar, to cool. It used to frighten you a bit as kids when the animals were killed. But there you are, that's what was done.

A SAD FEELING

I used to go to the Cattle Market with my father. Well he used to sell all sorts of things but he used to sell pigs. He'd sell a sow and pigs and sometimes he'd buy a sow and pig when the pigs were down by Newmarket Street.

There is less livestock now. As far as pigs are concerned the majority are reared on a farm and go direct from that farm to an abattoir which is quite humane. In the old days you might have a sow and pigs and you might take them to Market and I might buy your pigs and I'd fatten them and then I would take them back to the Market for a butcher to buy them. There isn't so much trafficking done like that now.

In the 1990s the pig market just collapsed and the pig keepers gave up. Pigs are a lot of work. You have to be dedicated. And the better you look after them the more money you make. At one time you almost kept a syringe in your back pocket. I enjoyed it while I was doing it, when we were making a few bob. But when we didn't, I didn't enjoy it then.

Before the Foot and Mouth the Market was thronging with people. Busloads used to come down from Wales. They'd flow through the market, go round the cheapjacks and take a look at the animals. Schools would come looking around. People didn't go abroad on holidays — Market day was the highlight of their week. It was a cheerful place.

I think what killed the Market was when they stopped the public visiting. After Foot and Mouth they shut it down and, in my opinion, killed it.

When I go down there now I feel a bit sad.

MUSIC-LOVING PIGS

One of my sows liked music, recalled *Margaret Bell*. She was crazy about music. She took off one day with the radio in her mouth, and all you could hear was this music going. She had this thing in her mouth!

Margaret Bell with her happy, radio-loving pigs. (Margaret Bell)

This one sow, she had 19 babies. I'd got no electric, so I had bottles in there to keep them warm. I stayed there all the time. And when they were all settled down I thought: 'I'll go down and get some sleep.' But I only had a couple of hours, and I don't know what it was, but I thought: 'I think I'd better go up there.' The mother had died of a heart attack. So I had to get the vet then and he said: 'You're going to have to feed them with this special powdered milk.' And he said: 'You probably won't keep them all.' Well, I was up there three weeks before I'd got them onto solid food. The vet called by one day and asked: 'How many have you lost?'

'Well, they're all there,' I told him.

He said: 'I don't believe it!'

So I was a mother to 19! I didn't lose one.

I always let my pigs out, running round the field. One pig, Nizzy, used to come with me in the woods when I'd be off walking the dogs. He would stay round a tree and I'd whistle and he would come to me through the wood. You'd hear him: 'thump, thump!' He'd come up and duff me one: 'you went without me!'

Then the pigs'd come in and settle down. They'd got a house with railway sleepers and straw on there, and I used to hang a sack down over the doorway, and they used to dive in there. And they didn't argue. Pigs will fight — I did have a litter that picked on one and killed it. What I used to do was get a tin, knock all the rough edges off, half fill it with pebbles, then thread a chain through and tie it up in their sleeping quarters. They would get hold of it and play with it like a kitten. You'd hear all these tins and chains clanking! They were happy.

I landed up with a thousand pigs in the end. And they were going out twice a week. I used to weigh them on a Sunday, mark them — the ones that had got to go — and then I'd get up early in the morning, about 6, and the lorry used to come and take them into Hereford Market. I'd go to Market, but once they were sold, I was gone. I felt frightened, because I was little, mind! It used to scare me because the sale was so fast. They'd have the hammer and they'd be 'blah blah blah', and I'd look at Jack the haulier and ask: 'What did they say?'

He'd say: 'You're all right, you're all right — they're making money.'

The auctioneer would be standing on these long scaffolding boards over the pens and all the people would be pushing around and the auctioneer would say: 'So many whatever-they-were pigs; now, how much? Start me off.'

People would stick their hand up, nod, or stick their thumb up. You got to be careful or you'd buy your own! Crikey!'

You got your money then before the next week's pigs were sold. It was always a cheque. They never gave you cash.

ACORN PIGS

I would take them to the slaughterhouse, but I wouldn't take them down to the pens. All I did was unload at the door. But one day one lot wouldn't go without me and I had to walk in front. I thought: 'I'm leading them to death.' That was the only thing I hated. It was stupid, but if something went wrong at home I used to think: 'you're being punished for killing pigs.'

I took eight in one morning, but around Mordiford one jumped and cut his throat. So I turned back, went home, and put him in a pen. Then I went on back into Hereford and the slaughterman said to me: 'You're booked in for eight.'

I said: 'Well, I know, but the pig hurt itself and I've took it back home.'

Because I used to let my pigs run and they used to love acorns, the slaughtermen used to say: 'Oh, here come those acorn pigs again!' But that's what was making the pork flavour. Anyway this slaughterman, he said a few choice words and he said: 'Well there's a butcher who's been waiting for these pigs. And he won't have anybody else's.'

PIG VERSUS MAN

There was a local character by the name of Cole who lived on Vowchurch Common. He won a professional sprint run at Edinburgh for a lot of money. But in those days, if you ran for money, you were disqualified as an amateur. Cole used to come to Hereford Market with his bicycle on his back and usually with a small pig in a bag.

And he saw Martin Pearson, the son of Mrs Pearson who kept the Market Tavern. Pearson had a piggery on Blueschool Street.

Cole and Pearson fell out over something and Pearson said: 'Cole? Run? I've got a bloody pig that can run faster than you. I tell you what, next Easter Wednesday we'll have a race from my piggery to the entrance to the football ground.' Between the pig and Cole. The news spread like wildfire.

Well, what nobody realised was that Pearson, with his cunning, didn't feed his pig, which was a sizeable sow, for three days. When they were all lined up along Edgar Street and they blew the whistle, Pearson had a bucket of pig meal up the far end, and the pig was gone! Well of course everybody closed in and Cole couldn't get by, so the *Hereford Times* carried a piece where Cole was beaten by a pig.

The Poultry Market

THE CHICKEN RUN

There was quite a big poultry market in Hereford. Different poultry breeders used to send their chickens to Mr Barnsley for him to sell. He was the auctioneer for the Poultry Market.

People used to come down from the hills for the chickens. There were thousands of the damn things at Christmas time. Hens, chicks and ducks in the spring.

The Poultry Market was busy on a Wednesday. When I was 13 or 14 I'd have a day off from school, or an hour or two, to go to Market. Wouldn't say it was acceptable, but I did it and one or two other people did it. We had customers who wanted hens.

I built up quite a trade in broody hens, probably bought and sold twenty or thirty in the hatching egg season, April and May. People knew I traded so they contacted me in the Market or the various pubs I used to call at and I'd deliver them on my bike. Tillington, Wormsley and Credenhill and Burghill, that was my trading area. Used to carry them in a box on the back. No problem. Father did make me a little trailer to go behind the bike, which would hold about four hens. We'd buy day olds off Barnsley one week, keep them for a month and take them back to the Market. So we had a cash flow going. And sometimes we'd buy more at the Market and I'd end up going to school with stuff on the bike — and be in trouble.

It was ok. Life was enjoyable in those days.

The Market place was the best place for buying and selling. During the auction everyone would crowd around Mr Barnsley.

He would be selling hens and chicks, month-old chickens, cockerels for fattening, or geese, ducks — depended a bit on the season. They were all live birds and it was mostly ladies that were buying the geese and ducks and month-old hens.

Haulier Don Gleed in a pony and trap at Canon Bridge with his brother. His mother used to take dressed chickens to Market 'and in those days they were dressed.' (Don Gleed)

Humane Killing

Father kept what he called 'scratching sheds' — they were 'deep litter' later on — and he always had about two hundred hens in deep straw. They'd lay round for twelve months and then they would be killed off. Those would be dressed. That was mother's part of it.

You buy an oven ready chicken these days it's just 'over ready'. My mother's dressed chickens *were* dressed. They took a pride in it. They trussed them up with parsley, sage: by the time you'd got the greenery off you got enough to stuff the bird as well.

Father did the killing. I did it when I got older, but father was good at it really because he was humane. A funny thing, a lot of old ladies used to do the killing. They used to hang them on the clothesline and they used to cut the vein in the beak and bleed them. If they didn't flap they didn't get all the blood out of 'em. But father used to knock 'em on the head with the stick. And then stick 'em though the neck and bleed them. Hang them up and bleed them.

We used to have a neighbour used to come and she used to say: 'Don't feel sorry for them else they won't die!'

At Christmas time, when Paul Barnsley was running Barnsley's Sale Room forty years ago, all the pig pens had a roll of wire netting strewn along the top and in would go live turkeys. There would have been about 180 pig pens filled up with live turkeys. They were bought by people who plucked them and then sold them on at the farm gate or into smaller outlets. Now you wouldn't have half a dozen live turkeys at Christmas — who wants to buy them these days? They want them all dressed and oven ready.

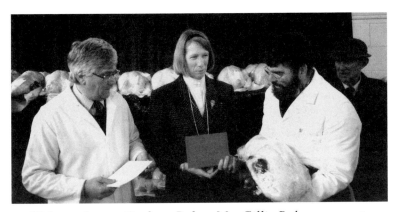

With auctioneer Graham Baker, Mrs Gillie Bulmer presents a prize for the best Christmas turkey to David Fletcher (right) who worked at 'Fishy' Gardeners, the butcher's shop on the corner of King Street, Hereford. (Graham Baker)

Paul had an old war wound and by the time he'd climbed up and down on the plank for about half of them, he was gone, so I'd have to finish selling turkeys for him. He used to take me back in the office and say: 'That was a good job done, would you like a Christmas drink?' And pour me five fingers of neat scotch in a tumbler. Oh my god. I'd have been about 18.

Up until five years ago the methods of taking chickens into the Market were quite extraordinary. You'd see a couple of pairs of chickens balanced in a sack on either side of the handlebars of a bike. No regulations in those days, free market.

Now animal welfare regulations are diabolical. I have as many as six officials checking up on everything that happens in that chicken market. We have a DEFRA vet, we have an animal welfare officer, we have a trading standards officer, we have the RSPCA, and a couple of others that I can't remember. I remember a guy who had a case in the back of his car and because he couldn't get near there, he parked his car in a car park and he carried the goose up loose in his arms. They prosecuted him for not transporting it to the Market in a recognised poultry cage.

DEFRA closed us down — here we go with regulations again — because of bird or avian flu. And they did it again when Bernard Matthews had its outbreak. First thing they did was close the Market down. Livestock market auctioneers never get any compensation like producers and farmers do: we get nothing. No business, no trade, no compensation, yet we still obviously have to pay staff, our overheads, rates. I asked Hereford Council if they would consider giving me a rebate on the rates on the chicken market while it was closed down by DEFRA — 'No, absolutely not, no chance.'

Priceless hens

When my father went to work at the Munitions factory at Rotherwas, we were chucked out of the cottage. But the Munitions had built some houses for their workers, Hunderton Avenue, Belmont Avenue and Springfield Avenue and we moved to Hunderton Avenue in 1941, recalled *Harry Carroll*. We had a good garden: everyone did. I remember all the vegetables, especially the runner beans. My mother kept chickens and ducks. Mother hatched the eggs in the warming oven and I remember chicks and ducklings running around the room. (There were rabbits too — they would arrive home inside my father's big overcoat.)

Mother continued working on the land while my father worked at the Munitions. Dents at Yarkhill was one of the farms she worked on. She loved it. She and the other women would travel out by bus or by lorry to pick hops and we'd spend our summer holiday going with her. The women would be quiet in the morning but would all be singing on the way home.

Mother's chickens and a few eggs went to one certain stall in the Butter Market run by Mr Rough — apart from other names he used to get sometimes. She used to say: 'That man said he desperately wanted some chickens last week. So I took him chickens this week and he said: "Do you know, my dear," he said, "I got chickens everywhere! Oh well," he said, "I'll have a couple off you."'

He'd finish off taking these chickens at a lot less price.

Indian killer

My naughty brother. My father had an Indian Game cockerel given to him, just an ornament of course. They're fighters. My father and mother had gone for a

Mrs Carroll, with son Harry, kept hens at home in Hunderton Avenue, Hereford.

A traditional Herefordshire scene. Mrs. Beavan (bottom left) with, next to her Mrs. Young and Mrs. Tuffley with the tea. At the back stand the pole puller and the busheller with the farmer, Mr. Davis in his best suit. (Margaret Wheatstone)

holiday and we were in charge. There was a lovely gentleman called Mr Walter Powell. He had an allotment right next door to the stables by the Market. There was the Red Cross Hut, and Mr Lyons had a yard with horses and then there was the Boys' High School along the end.

He had a lot of pullets, Mr Powell, so my brother who must have been about 10 got this Indian Game cockerel and put it in with the pullets and it killed all the pullets. Oh dear. My father was absolutely livid. Anyway Captain Clunes was the vet in those days. He said: 'That's a bit of spirit Herbie, don't you touch him, I'll pay for the wretched pullets.' Lovely old gentleman, Mr Powell.

STERILE THREAT

The poultry keepers used to caponise chickens. Do you know what this means? These little tablets render them infertile, make them get fat. And one haulier, his mother used to keep chickens and she wanted some of these tablets and he got them for her. Then there was three of us in the Dean Leigh café with our cups of tea. After we drunk our tea the haulier says to the other one: 'Tea all right?'

'Yeah', he said. 'Fine.'

'Oh, I dropped one of those tablets in there,' he said.

This was on a Friday. On the Monday the other haulier came to me and he said: 'He never put one of those tablets in my tea did he?'

And I said: 'He did, yeah.' I was carrying it on.

He looked really worried. And he said: 'It was all right last night', he said.

The Horse Market

Herefordshire was dependent on horse power up until the pre-war years. Hereford Market's horse sales were a memorable feature of city life.

Most villages had a blacksmith, recalled *Cyril Harris*. We mostly took the horses down to the blacksmith in Fownhope. There was one at Rushall and there would have been one in Hereford. If they had a lot of horses the blacksmith would go to the farm and give them what you call a cold shod. They'd make them at the blacksmith's and then bring them to the farm and put them on cold. But if you bought them to the blacksmith's shop they'd make the shoe there.

I used to take a day off school to go to the blacksmith's shop. Because, when I was a boy, I used to go down and help one farmer. If he had a horse to go to be shod he would get me to have a day off school. He put me on his back, just a sack to sit on and a bridle to hold on to. I was about 11 or 12. It was easy to get off, I'd just slide off. It was more trouble to get on. The blacksmith would put you back on, give you a lift up. That was about two miles and very often I'd go and buy a shilling's worth of cakes for dinner like.

You used to have Gypsies going around then and people'd always have four or five horses, wouldn't they, to do their shopping. They'd go into Hereford from Woolhope, which was nine miles, horse and trap. The people I worked for, to start off with, in the war, they only had a pony and trap. And they had four children and they'd all get in this tub, as they were called, with the little pony, and they'd nip off to Hereford to do their shopping. Would take an hour or more.

STRONG MEAT

Me and my brother went to the farm one morning to get the horses in, remembered *Tom Wheatstone*. Four came in, minus one, Black Bess. We found him laying down under a tree, not moving. Stan put bales round to protect it, but when I come back off the round, I went down to see Bess. As I got down there, the horse just keeled over and died. Stan said: 'I'll ring Ron Spalding.' Ron Spalding operated his meat business in Bath Street. You could buy dog meat in there.

Joe Bolter, landlord of the Brewers Arms, says to me: 'Tom, bring a couple of steaks off the rump end. One for me and one for you.'

I went down to the slaughterhouse and Ron was cutting up the horse meat, ready to go on the Paddington Express to London — it was big business then. Joe Bolter did these steaks and we ate in the bar. Off the same horse that I was stroking in the morning! Very strong.

Sometimes a farmer would sell a horse. They used to have horse sales in Hereford Market on a Saturday and sometimes when they'd had a horse for a number of years and they wanted to get a younger horse they would take their old horse in, sell it and buy a younger one. I mean horses had to work hard in those days. When they got to a certain age, well it was getting past it.

In the 1930s and 1940s McCartneys used to have a horse market in Hereford and my grandparents used to go on a Saturday. Local Gypsies would have been involved, they'd bring their horses.

It was funny to see the Gypsies bringing the horses in. The one in front would have his tail plaited and the head collar of the next horse would be fastened to the tail. They'd have about eight horses coming. It would be nothing to get 400 horses in Hereford.

There was the world famous Fayre Oaks Welsh Mountain pony sale and the first sale was held at Fayre Oaks Drive where Wilding Davies's Fayre Oaks stud was in Kings Acre Road. That was at Hereford Market for many moons and people came from all over the world to it.

On the Saturday morning in the 1940s there might have been 50 or 60 horses for sale there. You'd get a lot of Gypsies as well. After the farm horses, they'd sell riding ponies.

They'd have a space in the Market about 50 or 60 yards long and these horses would have a halter on, and the owner used to trot them up and down the road. In the market. There were a lot of farm horses to start with but there were all sorts of horses.

McCartneys used to hold what they call the sucker sale, in the autumn, which was colts, foals, which was quite big business because the breweries used to come and buy them to pull the brewery wagons.

GYPSY TRADE

There'd be ladies looking for hunters. There'd be a man called Tim Hogan who would come over from Ireland with twenty horses and stand in the pens, a horse in each pen, and sell them privately, what we call 'by hand'. Then there'd be Gypsies buying

Prize shire horses at a Show and Sale in the early 1950s with Ken Winney, Mr Bevan, and Mr Baugh. (Mrs S. Winney)

and selling and running and shouting and getting all excited and sometimes fighting. They'd be more inclined to be buying and selling coloured horses, black and white piebald and skewbald because they're very good in harness.

If you sell through the auctioneer you pay a commission: that's how the auctioneer gets his living. But the Gypsies wouldn't sell

A prize shire horse with Arty Mills in the mid 1950s with the old F.H. Sunderlands building behind. (Mrs S. Winney)

them in the ring: they'd have a deal with somebody round the corner and a few pound notes would change hands and that was the end of it.

RAGS

When I was about 18, recalled *Joanne Probert*, my father bought me a lovely chestnut gelding for my birthday. It was called Rags. He was in the stables in Blackfriars Street, but one Saturday Rags went missing. He was let out when some young bloods broke into the stables to get into the toilets, the hay lofts from where you could get into the football ground. When they found Rags he'd jumped some railings and run a spike through his hock. And we lost him. Somebody gave me a little carved wooden horse and on the back it said: 'In memory of Rags'.

Then in the War we had these two young soldiers billeted on us. They'd been through Dunkirk. When the time came for this one to say goodbye I gave the little wooden horse to him saying: 'This will bring you luck.'

The last thing we had was a card from the desert and then never another word. We thought, oh well, he was probably wiped out.

Then forty-five years after, my brother rang me up and said did I know anybody called Alexander? And had I given him a little wooden horse?

Eventually we met again and he bought me back my little horse minus its tail. The tail came off when he was in the desert apparently. But he'd kept it with him for luck.

Hay and Straw

GOT ANY STRAW?

We started with the hay trade. I was a young tenant on a farm and I hadn't got any hay and we'd had a bad hay time in Herefordshire, very dry, and so I wanted a pile of hay. I went to a farmer's estate and asked him if I could buy a load of hay. And he said I could have this 45-acre field. I offered to pay, but he said: 'Pay me when you've sold it. You're only a young man — you carry on.' I was 21.

We had about eighteen or nineteen loads of hay off it and I sold this hay round the Madley area to my old employer amongst others, and friends of mine in the Canon Bridge area who'd I known for several years. The next thing was: 'Have you got any straw?' It went on from there.

The farmers'd usually have load of hay to see them to Christmas then as March and April drew on they'd get a bit short of fodder so they'd come into market to buy a load.

On days leading up to market I would spend the days picking it up or buying hay, straw and some roots, like swedes, or mangels.

I have picked up bales of hay and straw and take them to the market hoping to find a customer. When we had the auction you could usually sell it. Russell Baldwin and Bright were the auctioneers, John Hawkins was the auctioneer, well respected in the town, and he didn't have many arguments. His word was law, as it were. He also sold the fruit in the market, on a Wednesday, 10 o'clock until about 1.30 p.m. and then he'd come and sell the hay and straw. I've sold fruit in the Market under him many times, apples and plums mainly.

Used to deliver hay and straw on a lorry. In the 1960s the bales were square, 250 to 280 hay bales on the lorry. We used to have to pick up the bales by hand. In the autumn there'd be about 130 lorry loads of straw and there could be 250 farmers looking for it. It was big business. I've been as far as Carmarthen after market on a Wednesday.

Hay and straw dealer Michael Ball from Eaton Bishop.
(Bobbie Blackwell)

Fire!

Mac Higgins was a huge character. He always wore a neckerchief that came down his front like a bib almost and always had a market smock on and great big boots and a disreputable sort of trilby. He used to stand at the side of the ring and if he felt that the auctioneer was going a bit slow, or he was getting a bit bored, he'd light up a fag and just drop the match into the straw and the whole thing would go up in flames. Oh my God!

Corn stooks line up behind the thresher on farmer Pearce's land at Vowchurch Court. (C.H. Davies)

Police constable 'Gunboat' Smith was about 18 stone, 6 foot 2 inches, a big lad as straight as a gun barrel. He was an old style policeman, ex-marine. Hard as nails. One time this horse-drawn caravan was tied up to the ring on the wall and Gunboat came up and said: 'Come on boy, on your way.'

'I'll go when I be ready.'

Nobody said that to Gunboat!

Next thing he's got some straw, takes out his lighter, lit it, and put it straight onto the horse. Away went this horse, clip-clop, clip-clop. Where he stopped, I'll never know, but I think he was practically in Ledbury before that horse stopped!

Fruit and Veg

FROM ORCHARD TO MARKET

At the back of the ring butting on to Edgar Street there was a great green tin shed all along there. It used to be for lairing cattle. We started a fruit market where we used to sell apples and pears and bedding plants, thousands of them every Wednesday. We used to have these 40lb apple boxes there and there'd be anything up to 3,000 or 4,000 of the things.

Produce sold at Hereford Market found its way into local shops such as Colin Smith's fruit and vegetable shop in Ross on Wye. (Colin Smith)

We had hundreds and hundreds of boxes of apples in the autumn. They were all from local orchards. I used to pick during the school holiday, before we went back to school in the late 1950s. Worcester Pearmains, pick those into 40lb boxes, and they'd be taken to Market on a Wednesday. People would come from South Wales, Gloucester, Shropshire and Birmingham to buy these apples. This was before the days of grading. You put everything into the box. One or two of the unscrupulous people would put the smaller ones at the bottom like they did with potatoes and the best ones on the top. People got to know because there was your name on the box.

Wye Valley Preserves, made where the fruit grows — Herefordshire.

Worcesters, Coxes, Bramleys, Blenheims, the old fashioned varieties. Golden Delicious wasn't even in the country then. The fruit boxes were all made of wood so they were fairly heavy to start with. They were open to the elements and the fruit was quite good. The orchards were sprayed, insecticides, so it was good quality.

The potatoes were just in bags. You took it that they were 56lbs; nobody actually weighed it. They were just open-topped bags.

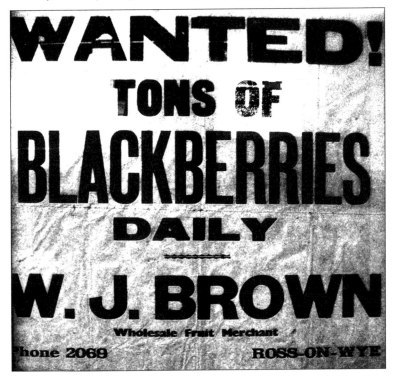

Fresh fruit — and no air miles! (Colin Smith)

CHERRY PICKERS

We used to grow cherries which we had to pick, and plums and apples. And you got to pick them with stalks on. Well if you pulled them off without the stalks they'd say you were 'plumming' them. I used to eat them — that was my biggest problem. Especially if you've had rain and they've split, they're so sweet. No, I was never much of a cherry picker. I did use to help collect boxes and weigh them, and put them ready to go. And somebody would come with a lorry and fetch them.

I can remember taking apples for Bulmers when I was on for Barwells. And they'd get a trainload of Irish in there, and these boys were unloading the railway wagon and we was carrying these hundredweight bags, the BOCM cake bags, full of apples, and there'd be that much left at the top where they'd tied it. We had no fingernails!

We used to deal with greengrocers and they were always desperate for wild mushrooms. We used to grow a lot of mushrooms. Father used to put as much as seven or eight hundredweight of salt to the acre to get the mushrooms. The greengrocers were always desperate for mushrooms 'til you arrive there with the cart and they were all: 'Oh dear, dear, dear. I don't know what I'm going to do with them.'

Cider

OH WE MISS THE CIDER

Most farmers had a few fruit trees that was mostly apples, pears, mostly cider fruit. Every farm had a cider mill and a press. I made cider. Sour old stuff. I couldn't drink it much. We made good or bad, mind, 'cause Woolhope were quite big cider drinkers. You put apples in the mill, didn't you, and a horse used to take it round till they were all crushed, then you put them in sacking or webbing, and press all the juice out. It used to go into a big stone hopper and then they would ladle it out into the cider barrel. Cider barrels were mostly kept on the farm. I have drunk it. You sort of want to sit down before you start it.

Cider making sort of started to fade out during the war when farmers were getting a lot of money for their apples from Bulmers in Hereford and Westons in Much Marcle.

Making the cider was a special occasion. You weren't allowed to sell cider because of all the rules and regulations so you only made enough for yourself. We stopped making it in the 1980s.

We had our own cider apple orchard, recalled *Rosemarie Watkins*. You just made how much you wanted and the rest of the apples

The owner of these traction engines, haulier Mr Llewellyn of Ross was contracted by Bulmers to take cider to London in the 1930s and '40s. One driver, George Stacy of Howell Hill, having stopped for water in Stow-on-the Wold, was running late and in a hurry. He was caught doing 21 mph across the Cotswolds and find £5 for speeding. (Colin Smith)

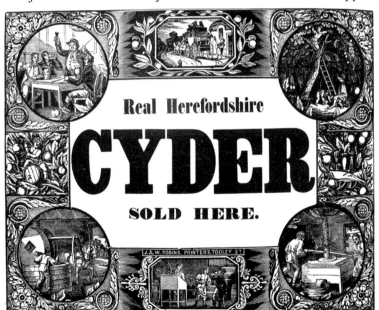

Real Herefordshire

CYDER

SOLD HERE.

J. & W. ROBINS, PRINTERS, TOOLEY ST.

went to Bulmers in Hereford. You let them fall and put them in bags. We had our own press. There was no horse to pull it around. I think we chopped the apples up in the pulper first and then we put it in the hairs. You spread it out and fold it just so and then the press would come down. The cattle had what was left. We would screw the press down with a great big spanner. We did it between us adding so much water. Then we put it in the casks and you had to leave it to work and some old folks used to put a bit of meat in it or a rat would go in there, to help get the impurities out. It tasted all right. Very strong. If you were doing hay making you'd have some then. But you didn't have too much because you were driving the tractors. I didn't drink much of it.

Mr Morgan of Woonton's mobile cider press.

Mr Morgan from Woonton was a cider maker. He had two cider making machines, one going round Lyonshall and one going round Weobley. He was a Roman Catholic and he used to start his engine up on a Sunday morning, make a noise — bang, bang, bang, bang. And then he'd shut the engine down and go up to church. Oh we miss the cider!

Cider Girls: Land Army women like Irene Hewitt and Barbara Cambell were sometimes given cider by the farmers. 'Somehow cider made the work seem easier,' recalled Land Girl Eve Lichfield. (Eve Lichfield)

Seed and Grain

The Corn Exchange was originally in Broad Street, next to the Kemble Theatre, with the Hop Market. Then it was moved to a big room at The Market Tavern.

The Tavern was kept by a lady called Mrs Pearson whose son worked in the Cattle Market, but then Sid Jones whose father kept the Imperial took it on.

The business of the agricultural merchant or corn merchant as they were called was very regional and a highly respected business, recalled *Tom Nellist*.

All the farmers would come in on a Wednesday to the Market Tavern. Every merchant had their own individual desk with their name on, which they would stand behind. Shirt and tie and jacket, oh yes. There would be around 32 companies there. A lot of shippers came from Gloucester and Bristol selling whole maize. You had lime merchants producing lime to go on the land. There was a huge subsidy on lime then.

You knew when a particular farmer came through the door which desk he was going to make for. There was a lot of loyalty. It was very Victorian, very orderly, very gentlemanly. Whole Herefordshire families would deal with the same merchant unless something went wrong and they would leave him. That was very rare.

In Herefordshire you could grow anything. And the beauty of trading in Herefordshire was there were so many different crops that could be grown. If one was bad the other would be good. There was never a total disaster.

In the spring you'd have planting of seed grain, seed grain orders, and fertiliser orders. There would always be animal feed orders right through the year. Then July and August time the harvest would start. Farmers would bring in samples which we purchased. You didn't analyse it chemically or anything. You just looked at it: 'Yes, the maltster will like that.' Or: 'The miller will like it.' That was it. You knew exactly what he wanted.

It was entirely dependent on the weather of course. If you had the right weather conditions you had good crops. The bad times were either a lack of rain or sunshine or disastrous harvest when the rains spoiled it. Of course then there wasn't the amount of grain dryers about to process the grain and keep its condition. It was a much riskier business.

Harvest credit

The normal terms on both sides were twenty-eight days' payment. A month's credit if you like. But when I started there was a lot of Harvest Credit which meant that you gave the farmer credit until he had produce to sell you at harvest time. You then contra-ed what he owed you and give him the remainder. Hopefully there was some left!

There was no such thing as a written contract. It was just 'a gentleman's word is his bond'. A shake of the hands and that was it. It never went wrong. And it was a nice way to do business.

They'd have a deal with a shake of the hand. Nowadays it's got to be signed, countersigned, witnessed in triplicate. In those days a slap of the hand and that was the deal.

We sold to the local farmers cereal seed, grass seed, fertilisers, feeding stuffs, and then we bought back their grain. That was then passed on to the maltster for making malt, feed wheat, feed barley, oats for porridge.

We used to mix poultry food, chick food, pedigree bull mixture and layer's mash in conical mixers in the warehouse. But then we had other stuff made for us, cattle cubes by a company at Tewkesbury called Healings, flour merchants. A lot of the cattle

Threshing the corn. Grindon's father, grandfather and the farm workers at Castle Farm, Lea, Ross-on-Wye work the threshing machine. They were terrifying contraptions and the rats used to fly out of them. (Colin Smith)

food was produced by flour millers to use up the waste in the flour process. We had people like BOCM (British Oil and Cake Mills) at Avonmouth — they supplied this area. You had Spillers from Avonmouth, Bibby's from Liverpool.

The produce would go down to Barry Docks or Cardiff to be made into either bread or animal feed. The oats would go to Morning Foods at Crewe. They still do. Malting barley would go to William Jones at Shrewsbury, the maltsters which became part of Allied Breweries. Malting barley would go down to Hampshire, Basingstoke, a bit would go to Eastern Counties. It depended on the weather at harvest time and whether the traditional malting barley areas had a bad harvest. The worst thing for malting barley is if it starts to grow in the ear, which is the malting process anyway. If it starts to grow and then stops it's no good. So if they had a bad harvest somewhere else then our barley would be in huge demand and sold all over the country.

Tom Lloyd combining in the fields of Newton Farm in the days before the land was taken over for housing. (A.J. Pearce)

Sun Valley

We grew and processed our own seed and we used to dress the corn with mercury dressings, horrible orange red stuff and the chaps would just wear a face mask. There was a lot of organo-phosphorous at the time which got into the food chain with the birds of prey and so forth.

We were ignorant to what was happening, but I can remember people becoming aware after Rachel Carson's book, *Silent Spring*.

The first load of ICI fertiliser to be packed in waterproof polythene bags arrives at Hereford Market in the early 1960s. ICI's John Roberts with Jim Probert of Church Farm, Weston Beggard. (Tom Nellist)

The single big thing that happened for grain growers in Herefordshire was Sun Valley, started by Colonel Corbett and two others producing broiler chickens at Shobdon. Col. Corbett was a Herefordshire farmer. He was a military man and had this foresight about broiler chickens. Then, of course, they wanted to produce their own feed. They started in a small way on Shobdon aerodrome then in a much bigger way at Tram Inn. The grain trade were horrified: Sun Valley would be buying direct off the farm and doing them out of a living. I remember a meeting being called by the merchants to try and stop them in the mid 1960s. It was unfounded panic. If Sun Valley weren't there now what Herefordshire farmers would do with their grain I just don't know because they probably take half of the feed wheat in the county.

Agricultural merchants visit the basic slag works of Richard Thomas and Baldwins Ltd., Ebbw Vale, South Wales in 1958. Basic slag was then a widely used fertiliser which carried a 50% government subsidy to the farmer. (Tom Nellist)

The Corn Exchange, Broad Street, Hereford as it appeared in 1858 when animals were still sold in the streets. A clock tower was added 20 years later. (Herefordshire Libraries)

The Butcher's Business

The butchery business was once local, loyal and centered on Hereford's Market.
But as one contributor put it: 'Ah, the good old days are gone. It ain't like that any more.'

HIGH TOWN BUTCHERS

Lots of farmers were butchers in those days and reared their own stock, recalled *Joanne Probert*. My grandfather was a farmer and a butcher, and my father was a farmer and a butcher in High Town. They would buy from the Market and outlying farms as well.

Next to us was Lawleys, and Gurneys the grocers two doors away. The butcher's shop was on the ground floor and went right the way back, with the offices and living quarters over the top. It was three storey. Most families lived above the shop. My father was the first to have a refrigerated cold room, a Hallmark, in the shop. It was enormous. There was an ice works down the back of the Green Dragon. The ice used to come in big sacks in great pieces which they used to smash up to put in this icebox through a big hole in the top to cool.

Grandfather would buy a bunch of cattle and then bring them down to Merton Meadow. There were big gates going off Blackfriars Street and then there was a big yard and open sheds where the carts used to go. Then there was a little row of loose boxes, not stables just loose boxes for the horses with a loft over the top that opened right out onto the football pitch. You could drop out of the loft into the football pitch next door.

When they used to have whist drives on a Saturday night at the Red Cross Hut they often got in on the hay in these loose boxes after. They had a fire there and we had a job to get the horses out. They went berserk with all the smoke.

EIGHT LEGS

One Grand National day, Gus Edwards, he was the head of the firm, he helped my father do the display in the butcher's window for the Grand National. They got a big plywood cutting of the Cathedral and a lot of this green grass and they made a fence and they got a little pig and suspended it from the rails going over this fence. We'd got a big doll and my mother made it a little jockey suit to ride this pig.

Daddy always tried to buy the champion beast at the Fat Stock at Christmas time although he reckoned he always lost money on it. The head of the Hereford would be scalded and shampooed beautifully and the shop would be open because in those days they had sliding huge glass panels on the marble slab. The beast's head would be suspended with all its rosettes on and there would be the little prize pigs at the back with oranges in their mouths and there'd be the hind quarters and fore quarters on these great runners running all round with their various prizes on them.

Christmas Fat Stock Shows were brilliant. All the farmers tried to win the top prize for Christmas for your prime cattle, your prime sheep and your prime pigs. There was always a lot of competition between a gentleman by the name of Bill Phillips and Derek Winney. They always used to try to get the Best Fat Beast in the market. Bill Phillips always used to be more successful.

They used to get their prize cards, 1st prize or Supreme Champion and we used to auction off the beast to the butchers. And when you'd see that at Christmas time, the butchers would have all the prize cards hanging up in the window. Champion beast, or 1st prize or 2nd prize lambs. You'd say: 'Ooh, look at all these cards this butcher's got!'

It was amazing how much meat you had off one animal. They could sell that beast over and over again. A beast with eight legs!

Allan Mailes presents a prize selection of Christmas meats at his shop in Eign Street (Mavis Mailes)

THE KILLING CRAFT

Everybody either took their cattle to be slaughtered or slaughtered them on their own place.

We'd kill one or two kids each winter on the farm. I remember holding the sheep while my husband killed it. And when you killed a pig you had someone come round doing it. You had to sort of set fire to him to burn the hairs off his skin. And of course a women mustn't help if she had her periods, no! They reckon it turned the meat bad. So she got out of that job!

Lots of butchers had abattoirs behind their shops. There was a man called Bayliss who had a lovely shop in the middle of Bromyard and he'd got his own abattoir at the back. Bowkett of Tenbury, they started off in a very small way with an abattoir at the back of the shop.

A lot of people had their own slaughterhouses. John Carver at Bartestree had his own.

In the early days there was an abattoir in Newmarket Street opposite the Market. And there was a public abattoir where the County Hospital is now in Stonebow Road. They were owned by the Council.

In my early days I would go and meet the butchers off the train and drive them to the Market. And they were butchers from Birmingham and Wolverhampton and they would get on a train and I would have to meet them at the railway station and drive them to the Cattle Market and then take 'em back after the auctions.

The animals used to be taken off the railway lines and walked across to the slaughterhouse. More than one occasion they've lost lambs 'cause they've run down the railway line.

In the old days the abattoir in Stonebow Road was very archaic. They used to put a halter on the animal and pull the head so it was down on the ground through a ring and then shoot it. A lot of blood. A lot of guts. Today it is much more civilized. They go into what they call a stunning pen. They go into a crush and a touch of the head and it's all done. Split second. And the sheep and pigs are done electrically.

You need to keep an animal quiet before it's slaughtered. That's why we always used to try and get the animals at night ready for what we slaughter tomorrow. So they're calm and they're chilled out. Because if it gets stressed, there's more blood into the muscle which makes the meat tougher. If an animal's killed under stress and strain, the meat won't be as tender as an animal chilled out.

A.W. Hartland's prestigious shop in High Town next door to Pritchard's Clothiers and Tailors, a business still operating in the city a century later. (Hereford Cattle Society)

A slaughtered animal, it's not alive. A tail might twitch for half an hour because there's air in the body and the heart is still pumping. There's air still in those nerve endings. That's why as soon as you've stunned it, you've got to bleed the animal because the heart pumps the blood out.

We used to have to save churns and churns of blood for people who used to make black puddings. People would come to the slaughterhouse from the Market, maybe they'd sold the cattle and they wanted some of the blood to make black puddings. Or roses. Best thing for roses is blood, that'll make your roses grow better than anything.

Each butcher had his own separate ear tag. So when the beasts went to slaughter, they'd leave the one ear on. They wouldn't kill them unless they were tagged. Then they knew it was JAP — that's J.A. Pritchard; CH which was Charlie Heggie; SOS which was Pritchard or an abbreviation of St Owen's Street. So that they knew them: 'Ah, ten lambs for Mr Pritchard of St Owens Street.'

LEGGING

The slaughtermen knew how things were done. We took Young Farmers in there and the slaughterman would slaughter an animal and one of the public health inspectors, Harry, he was a brilliant chap, and he'd stand there and explain what we were doing. All done the old fashioned way by hand. They eviscerated the animal, he'd show them what a liver was or what a lung or a heart was. You had the animal between your legs and you slid the hide off with a funny shaped knife, what was called legging. We actually had a machine in the end.

Father was also the first butcher to use a humane killer. But you weren't allowed to use it yourself. The manager in the abattoir had to use it and you supply the bullets and you supplied the humane killer. Before that they used to pole-axe them. And I remember my father, he was the first to have a demonstration of electrocuting the pigs. They had sugar tongs each side of the neck, because before they used to stick them. Ugh!

The skinyard was where everyone used to go for their maggots. There was two skinyards, Heron's. He had one down Commercial Road and one in Newmarket Street. If you were a young lad who

A family business, Rutherfords in St Martins Street in the 1970s. (Rutherfords Butchers)

would go fishing, you could go there and have fresh maggots — take 'em out of the skin! It was a very strong smell, very strong.

NOT THE BUSINESS IT WAS

A young lady appeared at an abattoir in Ledbury. She was about 18 or 20 and fresh out of college. The butcher was 65 and he'd been slaughtering since he was 15. She told him she was going to test him, to ensure he could still do it before she granted him another licence. He asked her: 'Have you ever killed a beast in your life' and she said: 'No'. He ordered her out of the office. But the licence appeared on his desk the next morning.

Eleven-year-old Herbert Cresswell outside the family butcher's shop at 16 High Town, Hereford. 'The family lived above the shop,' explained his great granddaughter, Joanne Probert. (Joanne Probert)

Butcher's boy Andy Rutherford. (Rutherford's Butchers)

Bowkett ran a very successful abattoir at Portfields where Sun Valley is in Hereford, but the Council pulled it down. They said Hereford didn't need one. It was a shame because it was so near for people to be able to take animals. The government wanted to do away with all these small abattoirs. Now animals have to travel 50, 200 miles to an abattoir. Some animals go to Somerset or Scotland to be killed. It's not good.

WET PROTEST

One of these animals rights lot, all of a sudden they appeared. And we couldn't get any stock lorries with livestock in to the slaughterhouse 'cause they all just lay on the road. They were bringing the cattle down to the slaughterhouse or the sheep. And there was

about 200 of these protesters, all ages. We had that many police down there in convoys and that. Then the boss come out. He said: 'What's going on?'

We tell him and he said: 'I'll move 'em.' And he went in the slaughterhouse where there was a big old hosepipe and he turned it on and washed them away. He got the cattle in, mind!

The meat trade relied on Hereford Market. Mr Mailes prepares pork cuts at their shops in Widemarsh Street in the 1950s. (Mailes Butchers at the Butter Market)

The Butter Market

A lot of the farmers' wives came into town to the Butter Market to sell their butter and eggs and flowers and dressed birds, duck, geese, turkeys, rabbits, and things like that. There was no prepacked stuff in those days.

In the Butter Market there were three or four cafés where you could have a sandwich or a cup of tea. 'Course everyone knew everyone else.

I used to bring rabbits, used to catch them on the weekend with a ferret, or in the summer time when the binder (that's a pre-combine harvester) was going round the fields, recalled Don Gleed. A gang of us used to go out on the fields, with sticks and maybe a dog or the odd gun and shoot the rabbits, and we'd share them out. All the boys did the skinning and gutting.

Sometimes I used to cycle down on my bike and meet at The Bell in Tillington, and then get a lift to the Butter Market with a pony and float. I used to carry my rabbits on the bike, on the

The entrance to the Butter Market in 1810. (Herefordshire Libraries)

The aftermath of the 1922 fire which destroyed the Butter Market. (Herefordshire Archive Service)

75

The Butter Market in 1860 displaying its new clock tower. Designed by a Mr Clayton it cost Hereford Corporation £1,000 to erect. (Herefordshire Libraries)

handlebars. Or if there were more, then on the carrier on the back with a stick across. Did it for pocket money. Well if you're short of money you'll do something for a bob or two.

We used to go the Butter Market on a Wednesday and a Saturday. We'd be there about 9 o'clock in the morning, sometimes on the bus from Tillington with your baskets and chickens. Live chickens went to Barnsley's, the dead chickens, dressed, to the Butter Market. I did all that dressing and gutting chickens when I was 11 or 12. There were about twenty tables, about six foot long, and you rented that.

My mother made butter to sell at the Butter Market. I used to help her make it, turn the churn, probably for too long! Used to wrap it in wax paper, in little square lumps. Half a pound, or a pound. There weren't so many rules and regulations in the 1940s and 1950s as there are now.

Some of the ladies were well known for their hats. They'd have big straw hats in the summer, there'd be the odd flower or two. Milliners were still busy in those days. My grandmother wore a soft felt hat and in the summer time a straw hat. Some of the ladies would wear wraparound aprons, some would wear smocking down the front like the butchers.

Mother'd be selling her butter and I would be beside her selling rabbits or flowers or eggs. Used to keep chickens. Picked flowers from the garden — there was no flowers coming from Holland in those days.

Drovers, Porters and Hauliers

The men who worked in the Market knew how to handle a beast better than anyone. Different contributors remember the tricks of the trade.

'Mac' Higgins, one of the last long distance drovers. (Brightwells)

A LONG DROVE

This man Higgins, his father was a sheep dealer, Mac we called him, he was M.A.C. Higgins. He walked a hundred and fifty ewes from Carmarthen to be sold in Hereford on the Wednesday. He got into Hereford, he came from, I don't know, Monmouth or somewhere on the morning of the sale, because they used to stop in those other places, and then they were there for the sale. And he sat in the corner of the Market getting his breath back.

But the sheep didn't sell. So he didn't know what to do with them. And his father was trying to get them sold. And his father goes into the Market Tavern and leaves Mac sat with these sheep. At half past eight at night he comes out to tell Mac he had managed to sell them. But there was a little bit of bad news: he had to walk them back to Swansea!

You'd have the auctioneers, the clerks, then you'd have the drovers, that's what they called them. Because they actually drove the cattle as they were unloaded, and put them into the pens. When the animals were being sold the drover went through the auction ring, follow these cattle round. And then you had one man penning them back at the end.

Martin Pearson used to pen all the sows and boars, which can be rather nasty. But when Pearson walked to put them in the pens, they'd walk along behind him. He always said: 'Oh, I've got a way with animals.' But when he retired, he told me: 'It's a packet of aniseed balls in my pocket. Pigs have a smell for aniseed, it's like a drug to them.'

THE STICK

You used to carry a stick for safety, but you weren't supposed to use it. If you could walk 'em up the alleys to the ring without using the stick that was what you were supposed to do. But occasionally there were cases where they weren't going to move or you had to use it for your safety 'cause one had to turn on you and basically defy you — 'I'm going to go that way'.

In the cattle ring there were some high posts which you could walk behind for safety if some cattle turned on you. You used to stand behind that rail and, when they opened the door after the animals had been sold, you walked back out and drove 'em on back through. That was the safety pen. If they started to turn or you got one that was a bit nasty, which was very often the case, you could shoot behind those posts and they couldn't get at you or do you any damage.

There are great differences in the temperament. Like with people. In the 1950s and 1960s when the Market was in its heyday, there was a great deal of different breeds of cows: Shorthorns, Ayrshires, Channel Island breeds, Friesians, all sorts of things like that. Some were particularly flighty. These Limousin cattle are very highly strung. I got thirty-two in the yard now and if I took you out there, they'd go to the far end of the yard. Now if it was a bunch of Holstein cows, or Herefords, they'd just look at you.

You don't hear much of Shorthorn these days. There were Friesian cows which had calves and there were Hereford cross Friesians which were black or brown. It's only in later years that you got the wilder cattle coming: when I say wilder, I mean European — Charolais are not too bad, but the Limousin, they're absolutely terrible. To handle Limousins and European cattle you've got to be young and fit. You got to be able to run out of the way! When I look back on my life, recalled *Geoff Jones*, I think maybe it was a good thing Foot and Mouth stopped me because I was getting too old for the job.

EXCITEMENT WITH THE COWS

There were some farmers at Hampton Bishop — Ivor Rogers, Alan Paske — who walked their cattle to market on a Wednesday morning. One dealer, Fred Ralph, who had a farm at Crickhowell and another at Moor Farm Lane would walk his cattle to Market and cause absolute chaos with Holy Trinity Church! Prebendary Snell didn't like them stopping there to use the public lavatory! But they all came and then the others came usually by lorry or they walked.

Father rented a wonderful grazing meadow at Lugg Bridge and we grazed heifers there in the summer. They got fat there without anything. And then we'd pick out the ones we wanted to take to Hereford on a Wednesday. There was no traffic you see. We might walk half a dozen or ten cattle to Market, a man in front and somebody behind, from Lugwardine, through Tupsley to the top of Aylestone Hill. We went up Commercial Road and turned along Blueschool Street to the Market. There was a water trough up

Commercial Road where horses and animals could have a drink if they wanted.

Drive 'em. Drive 'em through town. I've driven cows through Hereford. We had a small farm at Bartonsham and kept a bit of land at Whitecross. When I was at school father would say: 'Well, we'll drive those cows up to Whitecross.' For their summer holidays. 'Cause they were dry, you see. We'd take our cows that were not milking and we'd drive 'em right through High Town. There wasn't much traffic about mind. It was quite legal to do that.

We'd go over that bridge by Bulmers, then on the right as you go past Bulmers and on a bit, there's some houses with passageways round the back. A cow went up a passageway there once and there was some lady doing some washing in tub and she turned the tub over and got all excited about this cow. Really good fun!

When you're going up Whitecross you've got Baggally Street, Stanhope Street, all these streets going off, and if you've got somebody standing there, the cows'll keep going. They are herd animals so there's a couple who are always leading. But of course cows were kept for a lot longer in those days, have them for six or seven years probably, and they get to know the ropes! They know where they're going.

They're knowing animals, cows.

People would take a pig to market. They'd put a cord on the back leg of the pig, and off the pig would go in front, and they'd be coming round, holding the cord. It's how you take a pig to Market. And anybody who bought the pig, they'd take her home like that. Of course there were horses in trailers and stock wagons. In my time it's been stock wagons. Yes, I've walked cattle through High Town.

DOUBLE PAY

1954, I'd be 14 then, Fred Rolf, a farmer from Crickhowell used to buy cattle, either from Talgarth, Hay or up the valleys, put them on the railway train and send them down to Barton sidings. They'd travel through the night. Every morning on a Saturday I used to go down with Fred Powell and drive the cattle up through the street from Barton sidings, where Sainsburys is, up to the meadow on Moor Park Farm (where Moor Park estate is now), and leave them there over the weekend.

Monday morning, I used to go up at 7 o'clock, with a couple other drovers, Bill Matthews, Fred Powell and his dog, Bill, I think. We used to drive them down through town to the market for Fred Rolf to come down and sell them. I'd go on to school from there and then back after school to be paid. Rolf used to give me half a crown a day. Some days when he was a bit Brahms and Liszt, he used to pay me twice! So I'd get five bob! And if any cattle was left on the Wednesday, we used to drive 'em back up to the meadow and bring 'em round again Friday to be sold at the market.

Some of the houses down Three Elms Road weren't happy with the cattle — cattle kept going on their gardens! We used to get shouted at. You come down Whitecross, you'd got anything up to a hundred cattle and you got a dog there and you've got to run on and stop them going down each street.

DOROTHY PERKINS' LAMB

Reg Bayliss was a drover at the Cattle Market for over 50 years.

At one time, we had six lorries. Six small lorries like this one, taking sheep, cattle, into the Market or from the Market, into the slaughterhouses. Each day, there was something going on. So on Monday, it was always a fatstock day, where all the farmers would

Geoff Jones, left, and above the stock lorry he drove in 1950, Below, Geoff with his new lorry in 2001

bring in fat cattle, or prime cattle, prime sheep or pigs. Then all the butchers would buy what they wanted for their shops, and then my father used to take those down to the slaughterhouse. Dad took all their livestock down and it was slaughtered and then Bowkett, as it used to be, delivered those carcasses to the butchers.

There's so many closed down now. There used to be Mr Moxley, Heggies, Pritchards St Owen's Street, Philips and Preece in the Butter Market, Alan Mailes down Eign Gate. That's just the start: Rutherford, Pritchards at Fownhope. They used to buy phenomenal amounts.

When they were unloading stock, occasionally one used to get out. If livestock got out you always used to run to shut the gates. There was a lamb got out of the Market and it got down Eign Gate. Well, I used to work in the slaughterhouse and so I got a phone call: 'There's a lamb got out up Eign Gate. Go and find the boys in the van and fetch it.' So this lamb had got out of the Cattle Market, run up Eign Gate and for some unknown reason it got in Dorothy Perkins. There were two policemen outside, but they wouldn't go inside!

You can imagine now the lamb going round, taking all the clothes off of the railings. Well it could see itself in the mirror and it was ramming the mirror and trying to smash the mirror. You can imagine what a lamb does . . . all on the floor. It had done it everywhere and the two girls in the shop were stood inside up on the counter screaming. So we walked in with a wheelbarrow and said to the cop: 'Oh just hold the door'. We picked the lamb up, sat him in the wheelbarrow and walked him in the wheelbarrow back to the market.

But they have had times when they've had to have a police marksman 'cause some of the cattle have turned nasty and they've escaped. Because it's just not safe.

HAULIERS

Folks used to take the calves with a pony and trap. Later on you'd see a calf stuffed in the back of a car seat!

I was in school at Monmouth, recalled *Geoff Jones*. I was supposed to have gone on a bit longer there then but I was 14, school holidays. There was a job next door. The man owned these livestock lorries. His son had gone in the army and he'd got a boy helping him on the lorry. Then this lad left and I went to help him in the holidays. I liked the job and I persuaded my father to let me leave school and go to work. That was 1943.

In those days we'd be moving livestock, farm produce or moving furniture for farm workers. If a farmer had a worker coming to work for him he'd ring up and we had to fetch the furniture. I didn't like that job one bit! Hard work. You got to pack it in the lorry very tight to get it in there. People who moved furniture knew exactly where to put this there and whatever: we only did this job now and again.

I drove what we called Bedford Five tonners with stock sides on, not containers like they have used since the 1950s. Just sides that you fixed up. Safe if you had a load of sheep in there, but not safe if you had a load of cattle pushing. I mean, lorries didn't go very far compared with today. You could get roughly 60 sheep on or, depending on the size of the animal, ten smaller cattle or if they were very big, about six or seven.

The lorry cab was very sparse. Heaters hadn't been thought of. The only heater you got is a little flap down on the passenger side. You could drop that down and you get the heat from the exhaust coming in to the cab.

The hauliers in the lorries kept to their own territory. They never encroached on territory.

The farmer paid for the lorry to go to the Market. He had a bill every month or three months or whatever depending on how much work he had done. It might be once a year he might have a bill for taking cattle or sheep to the Market. And whoever bought those animals, if they wanted a lorry to take them home they would pay that lorry to take them.

The policeman he knew your vehicle and you could say: 'Jim, I'm going to slip for a cup of tea.'

'Ay, put it down here for now' or whatever.

If you'd try to pull a fast one on him, he'd got you the next day. I mean he knew his job. Like everything else, if you helped him, he helped you. If anyone was stuck, he'd go and see if anyone would help 'em out.

REVENGE

One drover, he'd do terrible things. He'd do anything! He used to drive a big Humber Supersnipe. One morning he drives to Bromyard and fetches his mate. It's early in the morning and his mate is in bed. He gets him out of bed.

'What do you want . . .?'

In Account with

H. NEWMAN

Haulage Contractor

SWEDISH HOUSE, STOKE LACY, Herefds.

Telephone: Munderfield 249

1970

		TOLL			
August 18th	13 Ewes x Hereford to Lugwardine		1	0	0
" 19th	5 Cattle to Hereford x Munstone	5/-	1	5	0
" 25th	Furniture x Ledbury		6	0	0
" 25th	12 Ewes x Hereford to Lugwardine		1	0	0
September 1st	1 Beast to Hereford x Munstone	1/-		18	6
" 4th	1 Beast to Hereford x Hampton Bishop		1	0	0
" 11th	1 Cow x Hereford to Hampton Bishop		1	0	0
" 14th	3 Cattle to Hereford x Hampton Bishop		1	0	0
" 14th	3 Cattle x Hereford to Hampton Bishop		1	0	0
" 18th	1 Beast x Hereford to Hampton Bishop		1	0	0
" 25th	2 Cows x Hereford to Hampton Bishop		1	0	0
" 28th	5 Cattle to Hereford x Hampton Bishop	5/-	1	5	0
		£	17	8	6
	Account Number 4845		17	19	0
	Rused with N.W.	£	35	7	6
	Oct 20" 1470				
	H Newman				

He says: "Don't ask any questions. You just come with me.'

And he drives to a caravan park in Worcester and they hitch up the caravan and they take it to the slip where they launch the boats in Worcester. Then he unhooks it and puts it in the river with a woman screaming out the window.

As they drive away, his mate says: 'What was all that about?'

He says that * * * * has been to Hereford Market telling every * * * * * I'm the father of her child. And I never * * * * her once in my life.

Phoenix Wright, a Forest of Dean man, was a travelling salesman in the 1940s for Torox in Manchester. He travelled the countryside with this ox-pulled van. (Colin Smith)

Doing the Business

Money generated by Hereford Market fuelled the local economy while a little luck money helped things along.

CASH IN HAND

The turnover in the Market at its height would have been £80 million. All that money was coming from outside the county: a lot of money.

At the Market the auctioneers paid us by cheque, we could have had cash off Hammonds on the same day we sold the pigs. And I think we could get cash off Hammonds when we sold calves in Market on a Wednesday, same day. But the other auctioneers used to pay the following week. If you didn't sell them then it was a disaster — you would get no money!

There was a toll you had to pay to the Council to go in the Market. There used to be an old guy named Percy, only a little guy, and he stood on the toll gate and took the money in. He used to work out how much he'd charge you for taking a lamb, or a pig, or a beast.

You were queued all down the road to get in 'cause you can imagine you only got two people on the gate taking the toll money. You had to stand there, tell him how many lambs we had: 'Well, I got thirty-five lambs on for so-and-so.' Or if you had a calf that was two bob, the old fashioned money.

We used to come in through the middle gate and pay the toll money then. A shilling for a beast I think. Sixpence for a calf, thruppence for a pig. We were supposed to have the money when we came in.

You'd say to the farmer: 'I gotta have the toll money.' It was thruppence for each sheep, each lamb that come in. I know some of them would come in with twelve cattle and book ten of them in so they could get a cup of tea at the end of the day! But they got wise to that, there was more cattle coming in. The chappie would come round and now and again he'd count 'em. I always tried to be honest, you know, because I wasn't paying for it.

Reg wanted a bunch of cattle this particular day and he said to dad: 'Buy me a bunch of cattle.' So they picked this bunch of cattle, 'cause dad knew where they were coming from. What did these cattle come to? About £4,000.

He said to dad: 'Come with me and I'll go and pay for them.' There was a long line of clerks taking the money and the payslips so Reg goes into his pockets and pulls this money out, in five-pound and ten pound notes and he pays them. And the clerks' eyes! Couldn't believe it! 'Cause he was paying £4,000 in cash! As he finished in one pocket, so he was going in another, and the clerks' faces were amazed.

LUCK MONEY

Our job used to be to go to Lloyds Bank on a Wednesday morning and collect the money with a man called Frank Robinson. This chap was a legend. He had a smallholding at Leominster and he came and worked for Alfred Hammond who sold the pigs and calves. We walked from Lloyds Bank to the Market with £5,000 to £10,000 in cash. The money was carried in a Gladstone bag.

We always stopped off at Higgins the pork butchers to get the hot pies and Monkmoor Street where there was a man there who made beautiful doughnuts. We had to get the doughnuts for everybody's lunch. One Wednesday morning, Frank went to Higgins and put the bag down on the floor with £5,000 in and walked away to Market with the hot pies, to be greeted by a telephone call from Higgins: 'Mr. Robinson, you've left the money'!

We always had to balance the books on a Wednesday night and Frank Robinson would always say 'weighed in lads!' when they balanced.

Everybody gave luck money. It was quite an imposition in a way really. It was meant to be a lucky penny and that, but it got to quite a bit of a racket really. The dealing men particularly would be buying things for other people and tended to pocket the luck money themselves. And could at times create bad feelings.

If the buyer bought so many thousand pounds worth of stock he used to get so many pounds per thousand of 'luck' from the auctioneer — luck money. It was an arbitrary percentage.

We used to say: 'No luck to anybody unless they spent at least £1,000.' Of course that went out of the window because you had dairy cattle making £1,500 apiece. You tried to avoid it as much as you could. But if someone was eyeing you and saying: 'What about it mate?' you very reluctantly put your hand in your pocket.

And then there were commission buyers. Practically no fatstock would be bought by the end user. It would be bought by a commission buyer who had been given instructions on behalf of the end user, which was an abattoir. All of those buyers made their living on commission (a) from the abattoirs and (b) from luck from the auctioneers. It was a very important part of their livelihood in those days.

The problem was that the wholesale meat business was always run on incredibly fine margins. They would be trading one day and the next day there's a huge bankruptcy. Suddenly you've got £70,000 or £80,000 and you find whoops, he's gone bankrupt. It happened several times.

I've chased money for auctioneers. In the early 1990s we had to take a trip to Belgium to chase this guy who owed money. I remember being camped out overlooking this bloke's house in a World War I cemetery, hiding behind the stones with a pair of binoculars to see when he was going in and out of the house so we could grab him. We got some of our money back.

DANNY'S SECRET
There was a guy called Danny Clifton. He died quite young, just as he retired, but he was a grand character. He'd been in the Navy, big strong man he was. I first started auctioning under him. I used to book for him when he was selling calves. I didn't know him terribly well but about five or six weeks after I started, it was a very, very hot September day. Danny was selling the calves and he was sweating like a pig, it was so hot in there. He took his jacket off, undid his tie and rolled his sleeves up and he'd still got his cap on, so I watched him and the sweat was pouring down. So I said: 'Why don't you take your hat off Mr Clifton, because it

will be a lot cooler?' And he gave me the most filthy look and told me to mind my own business and not to ask him to do it again. It wasn't until about three weeks later that I realized that he was in the transforming stages from being completely bald to having a wig attached. And it was to cover up the fact that he went from bald to wig that he wore a cap for about five weeks. Actually wigs weren't very good in those days, but his was as good as you could get.

DEALS AND DODGES

They've had instances where calves have disappeared. Somebody trying to be clever has pulled a number off a calf and stuck it on another one 'cause it's a better calf.

The Market police, the old fashioned ones, they knew the ins and outs of livestock. They knew the people to watch and who not to watch. They knew a bad dealer from a good dealer.

One Market policeman, he used to have a little Mini Metro. Well he had more kit to go home on a Wednesday night! Farmers would bring a bag of spuds 'cause he loaned them parking in the Market. He had his eyes open, but he had them shut as well!

The former Market policeman, Percy Bristow, foiled a theft attempt. This one day, it was Thursday store cattle, someone said: 'Percy, there's trouble. There's eight store cattle missing.'

I said: 'How do you mean, missing?'

So he said: 'They've gone. The pen's empty.'

But I'd got the number down in my pocketbook along with all the store cattle lorries. They got through to where this lorry came from and when he got towards his destination, he was stopped on the road and he'd got these eight cattle all on there. They were about £120 each which was a lot of money in those days. After this incident everybody realised: 'We're not going to get away with it.'

I thoroughly enjoyed every minute. Then I had the biggest shock of my life on the day that I retired from the Market. I was called into the office by the Superintendent, Stan Heals, good old boy. 'Constable, come to my office.'

I thought: 'What have I done now, or what haven't I done?'

Anyway, the Chairman of the Stalls Association said: 'Well, Percy, you're finishing today, aren't you? I'm sorry to see you go,' he said.

'Hold your pockets.' And he filled my pockets up with coins. The stallholders had collected them when I finished. It was about £19. By heck, I was a rich man!

There was a lot of trust in the dealing. You agree a price — thump! — and that's it. An auction has to be based on trust and when the hammer falls you have made a contract. 'I have accepted your bid, Mr So-and-so, thank you very much, £300 for that cow or whatever.' You are duty bound then to pay for it . . . unless of course it's got mastitis.

We did have one or two cases of fraud. People went off with cattle, people took cheques from the Market and cashed them. But it was rare. With auctions, it's only the auctioneer's slip that's written out: nothing else is written down. It's people's word. They go in and pay. I was always amazed how, over the years, you could almost count on the fingers of one hand the number of those who disputed it or reneged on it.

One autumn in the 1980s we had sold these cattle for a Hereford-shire family to a man from the Eastern counties and when he came to fetch them at night these cattle were gone, obviously stolen. We informed the police that they'd been stolen and I rang the Banbury auctioneers because I thought they'd be about the only firm that would have a sale the next day. A chap called Jim Watson there asked: 'What were they?' I said: 'Black cattle with white faces.' And he rang me back in about an hour and he said there was a bunch of cattle brought down there by somebody who was a bit doubtful. Could we get over there?

We tore down to Banbury and our farmer went in and, out of a hundred to a hundred and fifty black cattle with white faces, he recognised five of his. The offender got five or seven years for it. But that was one of the very few occasions, because everybody's looking out for each other. Everybody.

There might be a mistake about the sheep, and one man might think he's bought twelve or something and there's only eleven in the pen. Or a man's bought thirteen sheep, and you get 'em out and there's twelve.

You'd turn round and say to John or whatever: 'There's supposed to be twelve sheep, there's thirteen on there.'

'Oh, hang on a minute.'

We'd go back and check on the office.

'Oh, well the man only sent twelve in. Where'd you get 'em from?'

'Oh, this pen here.'

'Oh, so-and-so's short from the pen below. One must have jumped out.'

Course there's nothing like that now.

STRESS

There has to be a certain amount of stress on animals, particularly with fat stock, being loaded and unloaded.

When butchers buy a beast they hope it's going to die at 60 per cent of its gross weight. There were endless arguments about that from both sides: butcher wants to know why it's only died at 48 per cent of its gross weight. Farmer wants to know why it didn't weigh as much as it did when it left home. The reason being the beast was put in a lorry, came to Market, stressed, evacuates its bowels or whatever, and that's why it weighed less when it went on the scales. The abattoir rings up: 'Why isn't this beast dying at 58 to 60 per cent? You must have mis-weighed it.'

No, animal picked up, probably left in the Market for maybe eight hours, on a lorry for another four or five, put into a lairage with water, but probably no food. Or if it did have food it would be of a sort that it wasn't used to — you know what animals are like. So the weight falls off them.

But you'd get certain producers that were very wily and wise. They would shut the water off their beast twenty-four hours before they came to market and then an hour before they came, they'd turn the water back on and their beast would absolutely fill itself with gallons of water. So you'd say, a beast might drink five or six gallons of water – ten pounds a gallon, fifty pounds on the weight. That was their thinking. Not exactly fiddles, but sort of sly practice.

I'd never mention any names, but you'd get some old farmer and he'd be watching his cattle, and he'd be stood by the side of the scales and they always had these long sticks and he'd be leaning on it. You knew about it. You learned a lot very quickly.

Dean Leigh Café

There was always a café at the Market, but the original Dean Leigh Temperance café — 'Ruth who ran it with her mum were Salvation Army people' — was set up to offer Market people an alternative venue away from the demon drink.

CHRISTIAN NAME TERMS

The intention was to try and keep the men out of the pub so, in the old days, the ladies in there worked free of charge and because there was no wages to be paid they could sell their sandwiches and their tea much cheaper. Just at the cost of the ingredients. Ruth Morgan whose parents were poultry dealers and lived next door to the Fire Station was in charge for many years. She had about six or eight ladies working for her.

We'd get a lot of people in from the country on a Wednesday because it was a day out. It was the one day of the week they went out. Didn't go out any other time. They used to all get in the cattle wagons and come in, you know, all dressed up. The farming people used to be beautifully dressed. The wives were all posh and would come into the café and they'd look at you and say: 'Oh this chair's a bit dirty'. You never saw a scruffy farmer. The auctioneers used to come in and we used to just call them by their Christian names. It wasn't very often we used surnames.

The treat was to go the Dean Leigh. It was a well known drovers' eating place, and socialising place. It would probably seat about 100 or 150, 180 on benches in the winter time when it was cold. Good grub we used to get there. They started off pretty early in the morning, mind. They'd be there all day, the ladies, and they fed everybody, from the auctioneers down to the drovers and the boys. We all mixed. Bit of a natter, bit of scandal, bit of gossip. They had this old cast iron stove. Good women behind the counter who could cook well. Didn't stand for any nonsense mind!

The canteen was brown paint everywhere and a haven for us young auctioneers. We used to know these old girls so well that we used to pop through the back door so we didn't have to be mingling with the clients — you need a break from time to time. We always had doughnuts with our tea or coffee and we used to have these competitions — who was the first one to get sugar on their lips.

The 1970s were the good days. It was hard work, but it was fun. On a cold morning and we'd try and get them warm in the café. They used to come in and ask for a cup of tea and I used to say: 'There's whiskey in the bottom, don't tell anyone'.

Wednesday we used to start at nine and I could still be there at six and you didn't stop the whole day. We were absolutely shattered. I used to have ten gallons of milk on a Wednesday, early in the morning, and Ted Breese would always bring my milk in. Gorgeous man: I used to call him my teddykins.

CHRISTMAS CHEER

The café was dreadful to keep warm, very basic, recalled *Paula Smith*. There was just lines of tables, like looking out onto a school.

There was a red tile floor, which was awful to keep clean because there was all this cow and sheep muck everywhere.

We used to have two big sheep sales a year and in September the Fayre Oaks horse sale as well. That was huge. We had to get in very early 'cause they were knocking on the door at 7 o'clock for breakfast and

James Wentworth Leigh (1838-1923) was Dean of Hereford Cathedral. He was married to the granddaughter of the famous actress, Fanny Kemble.
Leigh was a Freemason who promoted the development of the co-operative movement, but he was also a teetotaller and a firm advocate of the Temperance Movement. The Dean Leigh Café, opened in 1915 and run by ladies from the Salvation Army, was named after him and provided subsidised non-alcoholic beverages.
(Herefordshire Archive Service)

then they expect their dinner and then they'd expect tea. You'd wish they would just go home.

The horses would come in on a Thursday and they would sell them all day Friday and Saturday. The Gypsies would have a roll of money in their back pockets and if they didn't buy at the ring you would see them come out and they'd be changing hands and all the cash was coming out. They used to moan about buying a cup of tea and a sandwich, but they'd bring this great big wad out of their back pocket and would begrudge giving you a pound.

On a Saturday when it was finished you'd sit down and think: 'Oh thank God I haven't got it till twelve months time again'.

At Christmas time the drovers used to find me a Christmas tree and they used to get a free lunch for that. (That used to be hell: we used to cook a hundred or more lunches for the drovers and the farmers who were regular customers.)

I used to take my own Christmas lights to make it look a little bit more Christmasy. We used to cut up egg cartons and my children covered them all in glitter and tied them on with the lights. And we used to pack up empty parcels and put underneath. People used to steal them but they were empty!

We hadn't been there very long and the Animal Rights came in. It was late 1970s. I went in one morning and the whole lot of the front of the café every window was smashed and they'd painted red paint all over it. 'Murderers. Murderers.' They said we were selling meat. We were inviting the farmers in who brought the cattle in to be slaughtered.

But when we had the Foot and Mouth that shut it. They never regained those old traders.

Pubs, Shops and Stalls

Hereford Market generated business for its cattle, sheep, pig and poultry dealers, but local pubs, shops and stallholders also made the most of the trade.

SPIT AND SAWDUST

At the end of the war it was very different. Some of the sheds were semi-circular galvanised sheds. The pigs went along Newmarket Street which was a single width road. All along the Street there were offices, pubs, the skin yard next to the Wheatsheaf pub, where the skin yard and tanners used to be. On a warm day, you'd know where the skin yard was!

Licensed premises were essential to the Market. It's always been said that you could not start at the top of Widemarsh Street with one teaspoonful of whiskey and double it up at each of the licensed premises: I think there were eighteen licensed premises in Widemarsh Street and four in Newmarket Street. The Market Tavern, opposite the pig market, was the Globe pub originally. It was a licensed premises of ill-repute, so I'm told!

They were spit and sawdust bars, really.

There was the weighbridge by the Market Tavern and the County Library just around the corner. There was a sweet shop run by Mrs Griffiths. One of my favourite was Cadburys shortbread biscuits. And cigarettes of course. We used to buy our cigarettes from her, not too many at a time because you couldn't afford it.

Wednesday, being Market day, was busy for Hardings. We sold everything. Everything was smartened up and put outside. If there was a frost for four or five days things altered. Instead of the rabbit wires going out, all the skates went out. There would be rows of skates, skates in the shop and Mr Cornack who was a buyer, it was his job to fit the skates to the ladies shoe. Whether he liked a pretty ankle or not, I don't know.

DRUNK IN CHARGE OF A MARE

The only pubs that had a market licence were within walking distance of the Market: The Oxford, Nell Gwynne which was the British Oak, the four on the Market corner. We all had a 10 o'clock licence, but on a Wednesday you could open ten till four when all the other pubs had to close at half two.

Different people used to go to different pubs. Certain cattle dealers would be in certain pubs; some of the poultry and one or two pig dealers used to go to the Dean Leigh. People used to get drunk in the pubs. Farmers would come home, people would put the farmer in the pony and cart, hitch it up, send the old mare off and she would find her way home!

I had to go up to the police station to unharness a horse which belonged to a farmer who was absolutely *kaylied*. The police couldn't unharness his horse. When the farmer appeared in court, he was charged with being drunk in charge of a horse and cart. He said: 'I'm very sorry your honour, it's not a horse, it's a mare.' He was still fined the same amount of money!

TURN 'EM OUT PENRY

Auctioneers had to go and have a drink with the boys after the sale and sometimes you'd get home. And sometimes you wouldn't. Very often I'd gone from one day to another without going to bed. One famous occasion we had a steak in the Imperial after Market was over about 3 o'clock and then got on drinking. My wife was holding a cocktail party that night and it's now come about half past seven and I should have been there half past six and so now I'm feared about going home. They said let's have another steak. So I said I'll have another steak on the understanding that you're all coming to the party. Well you can imagine bringing about fifteen pissed-up farmers and dealers back home for cocktails?

When I had a driving licence I went in one Saturday night to pick up my father and he said: 'You better take so-and-so home.' So I took him home and when I got there his wife said: 'It's kind of you to bring him home. He should never be allowed to drink.' When I drove back to pick up father the farmer was going up the steps into the pub! He'd got another car and driven back in!

THE WEIGHBRIDGE

June Smith's mother Daisy Jones was the official Weighbridge Attendant.

We moved into the house next door to the Public Weighbridge in the 1950s on my mother's appointment as Weighbridge Attendant. The scales weights ranged from 7lbs to 30 tons on hand operated levers in the office.

There was a garden at the rear that my father, Bill, kept fully functional with fresh veg, fruit and flowers. One side of the Market Tavern in the summer and autumn the Welsh buses would come up on day trips and in the evenings they congregated in the pub's big room. We would sit out in our garden enjoying the lovely singing next door.

The weighbridge was used for fruit and vegetables destined for the two local canning factories, hay and straw sold by the load in Merton Meadows, apples for Bulmers, swedes and turnips and the grain 'bulkers'. They even weighed each section of the new TV mast, made by Painter Brothers, before it made the journey to Sutton Coldfield, and two magnificent dray horses from the Cheltenham and Hereford Brewery, to settle a bet over which one was heaviest.

The taxation Department from Bath Street did their yearly blitz on heavy goods vehicles which had to have their tare weights checked and new vans and lorries were weighed in for their tare weight slip to tax ready for delivery. On the change of registration letter day we were very busy.

But it was all very friendly. Every year, coming up to Christmas, a bunch of holly and mistletoe would be left for us by one of the regulars.

When it was closed a new weighbridge was installed in Merton Meadow, a more modern dial-faced machine which my mother continued to tend. She was still working the morning before she died.

The amount people drank was indecent in those days, really. They would get helplessly drunk but they were never nasty and I've known policemen take them home!

There used to be a policemen Dick Penry. He was a man of six feet three, six feet four, a very, very large man, with the biggest feet I've ever seen! And he always wore his bicycle clips, so his feet looked even bigger. And there was an expression in Hereford: 'Turn them out Penry.' That came from when the landlord who would say at about ten thirty 'turn 'em out Penry!' And out they would go. Penry was eventually taken over by a chap called Gunboat Smith, who apparently had bigger feet than Dick Penry!

In the Market Tavern the landlady Mrs Jones did the most fantastic roast meals. There were two rooms at the back full of farmers and merchants. There was also the Victoria, just around the corner. There was a huge long table right down the middle and they used to carve the meat on the side. Sometimes they'd get a local farmer to do a bit of carving.

The bees' knees was the Farmers' Club which you had to be a member of. That would be full of solicitors, accountants, doctors, they all came in on a Wednesday. The place was absolutely heaving until the breathalyser came along.

COCKNEY PRIDE

There were the Market people selling cattle, but we were the other ones, selling all manner of things. With us it was furniture and china and all that. There was all this wheeling and dealing. People buying vases — 'cause some of the vases my uncle had were lovely, if you like that kind of painted thing — and then they'd go and sell it somewhere else in the Market for a profit, and that's how it all circled round.

Market Stalls in Ross-on-Wye. (Colin Smith)

The Market Tavern provided alcohol and sustenance for the farmers, drovers and dealer. From the 1940s it served as the Market's Corn Exchange.

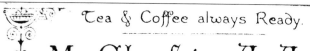

Eve Huskins, outside her home in Wormelow in the late 1960s, worked on the Market stalls for over fifty years. 'Trade used to be really good.'

We sold mostly three-piece suites — fifteen quid — beds, big old wardrobes made of wood, not plywood, big lovely armchairs. Good stuff. We used to go to Cheapside Street, Birmingham to buy it. We had a big Commer Cob lorry for delivering. If we sold stuff in Hay-on-Wye that wasn't so bad because we were covering that area, but in the Market, you wanted people from Hereford to buy, so you could deliver to the college or wherever. I enjoyed it. In a way the market was the hub of society.

I used to put up other stalls for other people. There was two real Cockneys, immaculately dressed. I'd never met any Londoners before and I couldn't really understand the way they spoke. They sold what they called these skeleton watches. They'd say: 'How d'you like this?' you know, in their London way. Then they turned it over and you could see all the workings; £5. £5 was a lot of money — I was only earning £15 a week at Burton's Bakery. They always paid me £2 for putting the stall up, and then a couple of quid to take it back down.

Then there was Harry, I think he was Spanish, and he used to put out all these tins of food and cakes and sell it like an auctioneer would sell it. 'Oh give me, give me a pound.' Inspectors used to walk round and I don't think they liked it so much did they?

And there was another man, a Jew, and he dealt in silver and gold. I'd have to put his stall up sometimes and he used to give me packets of fags, not Woodbines, but Players or Senior Service, they were the rich man's cigarette.

Crowded stalls in Hereford Butter Market

The Anglers' Inn in Union Street. In earlier days the road was known as Horse Street, a reference to the horse markets that used to be held here. (Doug and Olive Prosser)

CHEAPJACKS

It was a wonderful market. The farmers used to bring in pats of home-made butter, chickens, vegetables, flowers, bread, cakes, fruit, baby rabbits, birds, dozens and dozens of eggs . . . you name it, it was always in the sale. They used to hang dead rabbits, still with their fur on, from those clothesline things.

We used to have busloads of Welsh people come up in July. They would come up just to buy baskets of fruit to take back to Wales. You weren't just told the price, you had to bid for it. That was the best bit! It was just put out and you bought it. Of course it's not allowed now.

The cheapjacks used to shout. One old boy who sold crockery, he would smash a plate on the floor and then everybody'd look round and then he'd got their attention, hadn't he?

WHEN SIXPENCE WAS SIXPENCE

I was in Hereford Market on the Wednesday the King, which was the Queen's father, died. I used to catch a bus early in the morning and go and help a few people in the Market put their stalls up. People brought their own tables. There was a man selling second-hand furniture. He used to have a lot of tables and the person I used to work for, we used to have tables and we used to give 'em I suppose it would be a shilling for the loan of these tables. No roofs on them or anything.

This lady that I used to help came from Cheltenham and she'd have bric-a-brac, clothes, anything. People like the solicitors that used to have to clear out people's places used to get in touch with her. We didn't have no tills. When I sold I used to give the money to Elsie. She had a bag tied around her. Then with Betty, on the china stall, she used to put the money in a big enamel tea pot.

The stall holders they weren't local people, they'd come from miles, Brumingham. They used to sell all sorts of things: materials, very good clothes, cheese, home-cured bacon.

People used to come from Wales every Wednesday — you could nearly stand on top of their heads the Market was so full. Trade was really good. 'Course, I mean sixpence was sixpence, but you made money. But once the pits closed that really made a lot of difference. They started a Saturday Market, but that didn't start for a long, long time. Another thing that really killed the Market: when the car boot sales started. The last Foot and Mouth was the bug bear. That was the killer because the market was closed for so long. The last years you had a job to make money.

Foot and Mouth

Herefordshire's markets have weathered a storm or two: the Depression, wartime rationing, BSE. However there was nothing quite like the impact of the Foot and Mouth outbreak in 2001. It was not the first in the county, but the memories of market people suggest a story that has yet to be truly told.

THE NIGHTMARE

The whole Market was a fantastic place for agricultural business . . . up until Foot and Mouth.

This last epidemic was a nightmare. We've had Foot and Mouth in Herefordshire three times in my life, in the Market, but the last one was dreadful. We were paying a lot of rent to the Council for the Market. We asked for help over the rent but they said: 'No. If it's too hot in the kitchen, get out.' And the rent then, I think was £150,000 a year and the rates were something like £50,000 a year. I think we had half rates for a bit, but that was all they were prepared to do. We were eating into our coffers but fortunately for us, before that money ran out, the markets were reopened. We started off with ten or fifteen cattle and a few hundred sheep and I'm pleased to say it gradually built up.

The real break for the Market came in 1967 when it was closed for six months because of Foot and Mouth. All those people who had been used to trading on a Wednesday couldn't come in. They took to trading on the telephone which they hadn't been used to before. They got into that swing of trading that way and the Market never came back to the same extent.

NOBODY CAME NEAR

The first Foot and Mouth was up in Tyne and Wear at a filthy old pig farm. Whether he had it or not I don't know, but sheep from up that area were brought back down to this area. I had taken a load of those sheep to Ross Market, and there were thirteen rejects which I brought back with a dairy heifer. I delivered the dairy heifer first 'cos she was on the back and then took the thirteen sheep back.

The following Monday I was told that I had taken Foot and Mouth disease to Ross.

I had already scrubbed the lorry out with water. I was told I had to get disinfectant. I had to ring the Ministry when I was going to do it. I rang and said: 'I've got the disinfectant.' Nobody came anywhere near me. Yet it was said I'd taken Foot and Mouth to Ross.

I was worried about the farmer I'd taken the heifer to and I rang him every day to see his cattle were all right. He never got Foot and Mouth in the cattle.

I don't think one half of the animals had it.

But that was the end for me. I'd started driving in 1946 and this was 2001. This was 56 years. Yep, that was the end of it.

Mr Blair said that he wanted Foot and Mouth stamped out as quickly as possible and they put an awful lot of money into it. They employed the army to round the sheep up and the cattle. They had to be valued before they were shot.

I've seen grown farmers cry. They'd been milking the same family of cows for 50 years and they haven't got Foot and Mouth, but they might have been contiguous to a farm that had it. You had no option: shoot 'em! I mean a lot of farmers fought them off and barricaded the drives. But the worst part was they left the animals lying about the place, dead, for so long. On one farm there were 150 dairy cows, 100 other cattle, 50 or 60 pigs and something like 700 sheep. They were all shot one night and they were still there, all around in the farm buildings, the pens, ten days later.

I did 172 valuations and I did most of the valuations from St Weonards down to the Abergavenny Road and all the Golden Valley was empty of sheep. We started one day and by the time we were finished we drove back up the valley and we didn't see one head of livestock left at all. And in all those valuations — can I tell you the honest truth? I never saw Foot and Mouth once in my life. They never had it.

The vets panicked. Everybody panicked. They were horrible to the farming fraternity. Anybody that was involved with DEFRA should have been left hanging by their feet and dangling by the river. It was a disaster. And everybody got blamed. Except them.

A DISASTER

I saw the outbreak of Foot and Mouth in the late 1940s when Bill Gallimore and I were sent down to the Forest of Dean to do the valuations on the day of the slaughter. I met this chap one day and he said: 'You don't remember me.' And I said: 'No, I don't.' And he said: 'You're the bugger who took all my father's stock and your fee came to more money than his total valuation. My valuation was five guineas: his compensation was five pounds for two sheep!

It was very big outbreak, but the market recovered after that. They only slaughtered infected animals whereas in the recent outbreak they ring-fenced and slaughtered whether infected or not. It was handled completely differently. I think it was a disaster. It devastated this county. Absolutely. It never will recover.

I remember one man said: 'I've had the compensation. The cattle are gone.' But he said: 'You wake up in the middle of the night — silence. All of a sudden it's deathly quiet and you can't get used to that.'

After the 1967 outbreak they held a public enquiry under Lord Northumberland, but they refused to hold an enquiry this time. I wrote to the Minister and I said I think it was wrong. It was a disaster. They didn't dare have a public enquiry because of what would come out.

It devastated the farming community. It didn't affect all the potato men and strawberry men, but it devastated the livestock farmer. It's something they will never get over.

Kids love their animals. It was lambing time! I spent a week with one family doing their valuation. There was 7,000 sheep on the farm. And there were little girls from Bristol University injecting lambs, killing them all day and crying the whole time. And the sheep lay in the yard, dead, for eight days.

Eight days they lay in the yard. Sheep lay there stinking, smelling. And the family supposed to live there? Meanwhile there were these people telling us what to do. And what not to do. They had no understanding what was going on out there. Big men crying! And these ****** ******** saying: 'What do you mean? You've had your money. What's the matter with you?'

Later the Ministry were trying to get some of the compensation money back because they reckoned they didn't send the right bills. Yet they were importing men from Portugal and paying

'There were a few days when you couldn't see the roads for the smoke. The fields were full of menacing men dressed in moon suits. I felt they didn't want me to take photos.' (Hilary Smallwood)

them through the nose to come and do the work. We had vets from Australia, South Africa. We were in Ross on Wye doing a valuation and they had to go to Worcester first and get the instructions and then come back. And they were staying at their hotel, £120 a night.

ANIMALS ARE YOUR FAMILY

Someone rang from the Ministry and he said: 'I understand you have files and a dossier of things that happened during Foot and Mouth?'

I said: 'I have.'

He said: 'I wonder, if I send a van over, could I have the files? I'd like to have them to help us.'

I said: 'No. You can't have them. You can see them, but they don't leave my domain and that's it.'

He said: 'Well I think I can get an order.'

I said: 'You get what you like. You're not having them unless I'm with them all the time.'

We never heard another word. All they wanted was get rid of my files. And I promise you there is a story in my files.

People in high places they think, because the farmers were having a bit of money and compensation, that's fine. What a load of rubbish. Farmers . . . farmer's wives . . . you got big men crying their eyes out.

People don't understand, you see. You might be a hard old boy and you might shout at an animal or whack it with a stick or kick it up the arse.

But you love 'em. Make no mistake: they are your family.

Changing Times

Hereford Market has traded on the same city site for 150 years. The consensus amongst the marketeers was that moving the Market out of town was a mistake and one that would cost the city a way of life.

THE TOWN WILL LOSE ITS HEART

Hereford city is a market town. And to be a market town, it needs a Market.

They're gonna move the Market, but they're going to lose trade. People'll come to town on the bus and there'll be no Market. It'll be too far. Nobody will be able to go without a car.

I've never been one to want the Market to go out from the city centre. I was always very passionate about it being part of Hereford city life. And about ten years ago it all changed for various reasons. Firstly the wives, who would come over with the farmers, stopped coming because they're working. Farmers haven't got the staff at home so they won't come to spend as much time at the Market.

In the 1950s Hereford was a smaller place and then it expanded. They built new market blocks, new market places and sales rings and things like that. In the 1940s and 1950s it was just after the war, food was on rations and the government gave a boost to farming by giving the farmers a subsidy on the cattle that they kept. The Market expanded through the 1960s, 1970s and 1980s: and that was the best 30 years we'll see in Hereford. It's gone downhill since BSE and Foot and Mouth.

Hereford is noted for its livestock market and we have to keep a livestock market. But to move Hereford Market out of town will be a tragedy. The town will lose its heart.

The biggest change has been seeing the Market go from four and five days to two days. There was always a Market on Monday, Wednesday, Thursday and Friday, and then we used to take the Tuesday occasionally. So for much of the year, there was a market taking place on each of the weekdays. Now there's just two days in the week. Wednesday and Saturday. That's a big difference, that is.

SUPERMARKETS

The market structure for livestock is different now than it was ten years ago, even five years ago. Well, supermarkets are the cause of some of the problems. They're big buyers, but they want certain specifications for the pigs, sheep and cows.

It's a shame that the market wasn't redeveloped where it is. Most livestock markets around the country have moved out of towns to field sites on the perimeter of town, but it would have been a nice step for this city to have kept our Market where it is.

The younger generation don't want the market.

(Bobbie Blackwell)

Last year my son left the business because he didn't think he could make a living in the agricultural merchant trade for the next twenty-five years. That's the way things are going. Young people want a better life, more time for themselves.

Farmers aren't cut out with paper work. In the old days a farmer would go into a field round 'em up and run 'em off to Market. No licensing. No paperwork. It was so easy.

Now if you buy an animal and take it to your farm you cannot sell anything off that farm for six days. If you have a pig onto your farm you can't sell an animal off your farm for three weeks. You got to plan all the time.

There's been a general decline of agriculture as a whole, together with more rules and regulations. Some of them, the animal welfare things, were quite right. I hated seeing stock ill-treated or in bad condition, but the vast majority of farmers in those days looked after their animals because they needed to. Livestock was the farmers' livelihood. It made them money and if they were in a bad condition or dying, it lost them money. It was a simple economic fact.

There's talk of BSE again. From Ireland. That wouldn't happen if the supermarkets weren't buying in from abroad, from Ireland, instead of buying locally off Herefordshire farmers, or Welsh farmers. Because when you go to the likes of Legges at Bromyard, he's got exactly where all his livestock has come from, when it was born, the day it was slaughtered, you've even got the ear tag. These are particular to each animal. Everything's got this traceability about it.

Hereford Market and the Edgar Street grid in 2007 ready for redevelopment

That thing about passports meant that the whole dealing system and the turnover of stock just disappeared. A lot of people would say for the better, but a way of life disappeared with it.

Old cows that used to go in school meats, puddings and pies, all that's finished now. It was actually BSE killed the livestock marketing of bovine species and moved the bovine marketing to direct sales.

GOVERNMENT

The government, I think, don't want livestock farming in this country. Because they do everything they can to stop it. I mean: why the hell do you want a passport for a sheep? Why do you have a passport for a bloody horse? Why do you have passports for beasts? I can show you five lads who'll be coming in here for breakfast today and none of them have got any passports. So why do you have to have them for the cattle?

The man who, we were told, was writing the new rules and regulations for the movement of livestock in the United Kingdom came to Hereford on the train with another man. We very quickly realised he hadn't a clue about what he was talking about. He'd come out of some road department in the Ministry, he had never owned a pet, he'd never been abroad, he'd never ridden in a livestock wagon, and he couldn't drive anyway. *And he'd never been to a stock market in his life.* He was writing the rules and regulations for the movement of livestock.

Seems now, the rules are coming out. This Chappie, he's sixty something, he's been coming into Hereford Market forty odd years, and he's got to take a test: how to load animals!

I put a bull in with some cows: 'We'll put a lady on with him to bring him on into the Market. He'll be quiet.' Which it did do.

''Course I hadn't done it like the book says. And I said: 'Who done the book then?'

And they said: 'London, the book come from.' A lot of them don't know the animals. The government don't make any sense, do they?

Everybody just gets so fed up with having to dot the 'i's and cross the 't's as far as the regulations are concerned. There doesn't seem to be a great deal of common sense involved in policing:

A guy brought a cock pheasant in and it had been running with 25 pheasant hens and it was looking a bit sorry for itself. Their long tail gets broken because they have been busy and it looked a bit bedraggled, but it was perfectly healthy. The young lady from animal welfare or whatever decided that it wasn't in a fit state to be marketed, so she said: 'I'm to call the vet and have it put down.' The callout fee was going to be £25-30 so the bloke said: 'I'll soon fix that.' He pulled it out and wrung its neck in front of her. Which of course is perfectly legal.

I've seen the best years of the Market and I'm glad in a way that I got out when I did. It was getting pretty rocky then, but it's got worse since. Very sad.